PRAISE FOR *PRO*

We all know that the Book of Prove it extracting the nuggets can be confusing. Help is on the way! Dr. Coe has hit a home run. His directions on how to use and teach this Bible study are clear and precise. His idea of categorizing individual proverbs by means of the Ten Commandments is brilliant. Thoroughly biblical and confessionally Lutheran, this study is a gift to all who long to incorporate more biblical wisdom into their lives.

Rev. Dr. Reed Lessing, Professor of Theology and Ministry,
Concordia University, St. Paul

Reading the Book of Proverbs can be challenging for most people. The diversity of proverbs can lead to distraction. In *Provoking Proverbs*, David Coe offers readers an easy-to-use guide. He categorizes the proverbs according to the Ten Commandments, helping readers meditate on God's Word and be drawn deeper into the goodness of God's design. His questions, reflections, and exercises promote active learning and a personal delight in the things of God.

Rev. Dr. David Schmitt, The Gregg H. Benidt Memorial Chair
in Homiletics and Literature, Concordia Seminary, St. Louis

Provoking Proverbs presents the proverbs with catechetical richness and rhetorical verve. Its prose pops, its preaching pricks the conscience, and it always points to Wisdom Incarnate, who kept the commandments for us. It will deepen your appreciation of the proverbs, your understanding of the Ten Commandments, and your faith in your Savior.

Rev. Dr. David Loy, Professor of Philosophy, Theology, and Ethics,
Concordia University Irvine

One of the miraculous qualities of God's Word is how it consists of many different kinds of writings, and yet they all fit together perfectly. In *Provoking Proverbs*, David Coe sorts out the Book of Proverbs according to the Ten Commandments. The result is brilliant illumination. This is not just a commentary but also a Bible study. Writing in an engaging style, leavened with wit as well as wisdom, Professor Coe has devised a lively, stimulating, and thorough framework for reflection and discussion. His book is a model of how to teach Law and Gospel.

Gene Edward Veith Jr., PhD, author of *The Spirituality of the Cross*

Provoking Proverbs . . . is a splendid invitation to enter the world of Old Testament wisdom. By placing select proverbs into the context of the Ten Commandments, Dr. Coe offers a fresh appropriation and reading of texts that are sometimes passed over only superficially. . . . This volume does a great service in demonstrating how the proverbs flow from and are based on the larger theological vision of the Old Testament. The bridges that are built—linking proverbs to the Ten Commandments—display faithfulness to Sacred Scripture and to the Lutheran Confessions. Lutheran categories punctuate the treatment of texts and enrich this study significantly. Finally, a feature that should attract wide usage is the very practical emphasis. Practical guidelines include helpful tips such as Think and Ink, Mark and Remark, and Personalize and Memorize. Throughout *Provoking Proverbs*, there are insightful pedagogical suggestions. Here substantive scriptural theology is combined with a very practical goal—faithful Christian living. May this volume, by God's grace, provoke just such an outcome.

Rev. Dr. Dean Wenthe, President of the Concordia University System, Professor of Exegetical Theology, and President Emeritus of Concordia Theological Seminary, Fort Wayne

David Coe helps us to mine the treasure trove of wisdom in the Book of Proverbs. The way in which he categorizes the proverbs according to the Ten Commandments enables the reader to integrate their message and apply their meaning to real life. Coe brings seasoned theological insight to guide us to respond in sanctified action. Blessed is the one who walks in the counsel of this book!

Rev. Dr. David Peter, Professor of Practical Theology and Dean of Faculty, Concordia Seminary, St. Louis

Drawing deep from the well—not just of Proverbs, but of the whole Bible—this study will refresh your soul. It satisfies not only because it's delightfully worded and stylistically succinct but also because Professor Coe coaches us how to soak in God's personal Wisdom, infused in each of the Ten Commandments, dripping from every proverb, and incarnate in Jesus for the life of the world. Follow this plan once (or repeatedly) and you will have a new set of personalized, memorized proverbs, carefully filtered through the Gospel, "like cold water to a thirsty soul" (Proverbs 25:25).

Rev. Dr. Michael Zeigler, Speaker of *The Lutheran Hour*, Lutheran Hour Ministries

PROVOKING PROVERBS

Wisdom and the Ten Commandments

DAVID LAWRENCE COE

CONCORDIA PUBLISHING HOUSE • SAINT LOUIS

Published by Concordia Publishing House
3558 S. Jefferson Avenue, St. Louis, MO 63118-3968
1-800-325-3040 • cph.org

Manufactured in the United States of America

Library of Congress Cataloging-in-Publication Data

Names: Coe, David Lawrence, author.

Title: Provoking Proverbs / David Lawrence Coe.

Description: Saint Louis, MO : Concordia Publishing House, 2020. | Summary:
"In this Bible study, Dr. Coe explains and categorizes the
Proverbs according to the Ten Commandments. Readers (college age and
adults) will gain a new understanding of how this book of the Bible
guides us in our everyday life"-- Provided by publisher.

Identifiers: LCCN 2020022113 (print) | LCCN 2020022114 (ebook) | ISBN
9780758667434 (paperback) | ISBN 9780758667441 (ebook)

Subjects: LCSH: Bible. Proverbs--Textbooks.

Classification: LCC BS1467 .C64 2020 (print) | LCC BS1467 (ebook) | DDC
223/.70071--dc23

LC record available at https://lccn.loc.gov/2020022113

LC ebook record available at https://lccn.loc.gov/2020022114

1 2 3 4 5 6 7 8 9 10   29 28 27 26 25 24 23 22 21 20

CONTENTS

To Samuel and Caleb

Incline your ear, and hear the words of the wise,
and apply your heart to my knowledge,
for it will be pleasant if you keep them within you,
if all of them are ready on your lips.

PROVERBS 22:17–18

READER TIPS

This Bible study categorizes the proverbs of the Book of Proverbs according to the Ten Commandments so that you can easily analyze, personalize, and memorize your top ten favorite biblical proverbs—one for each of the Ten Commandments—provoking you to fear, love, and trust in God above all things because God forgives, loves, and treasures you first (1 John 4:19). Get ready to get poked and provoked by *Provoking Proverbs!* Here are some tips as you read this study:

- You can use this book on your own or with a group.

- This study categorizes the proverbs of the Book of Proverbs according to the commandment each proverb speaks of keeping or breaking. For example, "Whoever gives an honest answer kisses the lips" (Proverbs 24:26) keeps the Eighth Commandment, while "As charcoal to hot embers and wood to fire, so is a quarrelsome man for kindling strife" (Proverbs 26:21) breaks it.

- A popular proverb introduces each category of biblical proverbs. For example, the proverb "Words once spoken you can never recall" introduces all the Eighth Commandment proverbs on hurting our neighbor's reputation; "Honey catches more flies than vinegar" introduces all of the proverbs that touch on explaining everything in the kindest way. This exemplifies that the Law of God is written on the heart (Romans 2:14–15) and that worldly wisdom and biblical wisdom often say the same thing when it comes to the Law.

- The most perplexing proverbs are footnoted with explanations. Thankfully, most of the biblical proverbs are common sense and not rocket science. Consult *The Lutheran Study Bible* when needed.

- Sometimes, footnotes reference the Lutheran Confessions, the documents that explain what Lutherans believe according to the Bible. If you're interested in learning more about a topic, consider looking up the reference in *Concordia: The Lutheran Confessions*. The Confessions will point you to Scripture and help explain the topic.

- Questions are scattered throughout each chapter and identified as Deep Memory, Think and Ink, Pair and Share, Mark and Remark, or Personalize and Memorize.

  - Deep Memory asks you to dig deep in your memory and ink the main points you previously learned.

  - Think and Ink asks you to quietly think and ink an answer for yourself.

- Pair and Share asks you to pair up with a neighbor and share an answer. If you are reading *Provoking Proverbs* privately, treat Pair and Share questions as Think and Ink questions.

- Mark and Remark comes at the end of a proverb category. Analyze all the proverbs you just read, mark your favorite, and remark why you chose it.

- Personalize and Memorize comes at the end of each chapter. Analyze all the proverbs you previously marked from the Mark and Remark sections, choose your personal favorite, and memorize it. This proverb is your favorite proverb for that commandment. When you finish the study, you'll have your top ten proverbs from the Book of Proverbs, one for each of the Ten Commandments.

- Check out the Answer Guide in the back of the book for answers to the numbered questions from each chapter.

- The Summary Sheet in the back of the book invites you to ink your favorite proverbs from the Book of Proverbs one last time, one for each of the Ten Commandments. This will sum up everything you learned on one sheet, jog your memory for years to come, and provoke you to fear, love, and trust in God today and tomorrow because God forgives, loves, and treasures you first (1 John 4:19).

LEADER TIPS

Pastors, teachers, and leaders can use *Provoking Proverbs* any time they want to teach the Book of Proverbs, the Ten Commandments, biblical ethics, confirmation, or college faith-and-life courses with passion and power. Here are some tips as you lead this study:

- Make sure to read the Reader Tips before you read the rest of these Leader Tips.

- Invite participants to peruse the preface before your first meeting. Depending on the time you have, you can use the preface as its own lesson or just briefly go over it before diving into the first chapter.

- To shorten the study, consider combining some of the chapters, such as the chapters on the Ninth and Tenth Commandments. The chapters on the Second and Tenth Commandments are fairly short and could be explored independently by participants.

- Take turns reading each proverb out loud. Ask the person at the beginning of a row to read the first proverb. Then, the next person *immediately* reads the second proverb, and so on to the end of the category. This recited rhythm is the heartbeat of the study. Reciting several proverbs that convey the same conviction in different ways cuts to the chase and cuts to the heart (Acts 2:37). You'll hear participants blurt "Whoa!" and "Hmm!" as God's proverbs do their provoking work.

- Examine each chapter before each lesson to ensure you understand each proverb. Consult *The Lutheran Study Bible* when necessary.

- Feel free to omit any of the questions scattered throughout each chapter, especially if time is short.

- Give thirty seconds to one minute for participants to answer each question.

- Invite two to three people to share an answer, and share your own sometimes. Vary the respondents to keep the lesson moving.

- Go out with a bang! For the Personalize and Memorize question at the end of each chapter, invite as many participants as possible to quickly proclaim their favorite proverb from the chapter like fireworks, one after another.

- Close the lesson with prayer. A printed prayer concludes each chapter, or you can close with your own.

- *Provoking Proverbs* also serves as a handy categorized index of almost all of the Book of Proverbs. For example, when it's time to lay down the Law before you give out the Gospel, proclaiming three to five provoking proverbs in a row on the same sin cuts to the chase and cuts to the heart (Acts 2:37).

- If you ever need to lead a short devotion, *Provoking Proverbs* can be a helpful collection. Each category of proverbs may serve as one short devotion. For example, you could turn to the Fourth Commandment category entitled "Two Heads Are Better Than One" on the wisdom of being teachable and amenable. Read the introduction to that category, take turns reading each proverb from the category, and invite participants to mark their favorite proverb from the ones they just read and remark why they chose it. The prayer at the end of the corresponding chapter may be used as your closing prayer.

PREFACE

Incline your ear, and hear the words of the wise,
and apply your heart to my knowledge,
for it will be pleasant if you keep them within you,
if all of them are ready on your lips.

PROVERBS 22:17–18

There's More Than One Way to Skin a Cat

What did your momma used to say? When I needed help completing a tough fourth-grade project on the assassination of Abraham Lincoln, Momma counseled, "There's more than one way to skin a cat." At ten years old, I felt a little weird imagining our cat, Fluffy, getting skinned. But even at ten, I was intuitive enough to know what Momma meant—"There is more than one way to complete this project"—and she had confidence I could think through my options to choose the most effective and efficient way for myself. Mom's pithy proverb graciously brought both truth and humor to my preadolescent problem, giving me the heart to press on and the wisdom to not take myself too seriously.

Pair and Share

1. What's your favorite nonbiblical proverb? Here are some examples: There's more than one way to skin a cat. The early bird gets the worm. Lie down with dogs, wake up with fleas.

The Best Things Come in Small Packages

Popular proverbs like these—"Curiosity killed the cat," "When the cat's away, the mice will play"—are also known as wise sayings, adages, aphorisms, apothegms, axioms, maxims, morals, mottoes, street smarts, worldly wisdom, and just plain old common sense. Proverbs 1 depicts proverbs as the words of the wise for the instruction of the young and anyone wise enough to listen and learn:

> 1:1 The proverbs of Solomon, son of David, king of Israel:
>
> 2 To know wisdom and instruction,
>> to understand words of insight,
>
> 3 to receive instruction in wise dealing,
>> In righteousness, justice, and equity;
>
> 4 to give prudence to the simple,
>> knowledge and discretion to the youth—
>
> 5 Let the wise hear and increase in learning,
>> and the one who understands obtain guidance,
>
> 6 to understand a proverb and a saying,
>> the words of the wise and their riddles.

Think and Ink

2. What is a proverb? Put Proverbs 1:1–6 in your own words. Sum it all up with a pithy sentence.

Proverbs are profound; they pack a lot of wisdom in one wallop. Whether it's a popular proverb like "Honey catches more flies than vinegar" or a biblical proverb like "Gracious words are like a honeycomb, sweetness to the soul and health to the body" (Proverbs 16:24), it incisively informs that kindness and gentleness are more effective than crudeness and rudeness. All proverbs are fun, memorable, short, pithy statements that state a general truth (such as "Time flies"), give good advice (such as "Take it one day at a time"), or both (such as "A stitch in time saves nine").

Nothing Hurts Like the Truth

Yes, proverbs are profound, but proverbs can also be provoking. The Old Testament Book of Proverbs is a provoking book of Law, telling us what to do and what not to do. Not just a list of no-nos and dos and don'ts, God's Law commands what God demands and cans what God bans. Although original sin has infected and defected our knowledge of the Law,[1] Paul says that the Law of God is written on our hearts (Romans 2:14–15). You're most likely like me: my conscience accuses me when I lean toward what's wrong and excuses me when I lean toward what's right. Many philosophers refer to this natural knowledge of morality as natural law, a moral order built into human nature, not conditioned by culture. Everyone everywhere naturally knows that murder, adultery, theft, and the rest are wrong. Why is our conscience haunted by this natural knowledge of right and wrong? Conditioned by culture, we say, "Because we were raised that way," but the Bible says it's ultimately because we were built that way (Romans 2:14–15). Yes, original sin has waned and weakened the natural knowledge of God's Law written on our hearts, but God's Law still has the power to poke and provoke everyone everywhere, whether we are Christian or non-Christian, African or Asian, eighteen or eighty-two.

Think and Ink

3. Read Romans 2:14–15. When was the last time your conscience accused you or excused you? What happened?

Tell Me Something I Don't Know

Since the Book of Proverbs is a book of Law and the Law of God is still written on our hard-hearted hearts, Proverbs is full of provocations that our heads have a hint are true and that our hearts aren't always happy to hear. When I was sixteen and whining about a summertime job I didn't want to do, my daddy told me, "A cat in gloves catches no mice." Deep down, before Dad said that, I already knew that if I wanted to achieve anything meaningful, I was going to have to get my hands dirty. Proverbs 14:4 says the same: "Where there are no oxen, the manger is clean, but abundant crops come by the strength of the ox."

---

[1] Solid Declaration I 12.

The power of proverbs, whether biblical or popular, is not that they provide new knowledge; instead, their power is to poke and provoke. Yes, I already knew I was going to have to get my hands dirty if I wanted to achieve anything meaningful, but when Dad said, "A cat in gloves catches no mice," he poked me in the pathos with the gentle power of a proverb.[2] On one hand, Dad's proverb was *provoking*; it got under my skin and confronted my laziness. On the other, his proverb was *thought-provoking*; it made me imagine myself as a finicky cat with a wriggly-wiggly mouse to catch. Dad's proverb, both serious and humorous, put me at ease and gave me the gumption to consider myself from a more lighthearted perspective. The Book of Proverbs pokes and provokes the same way: "Go to the ant, O sluggard; consider her ways, and be wise. Without having any chief, officer, or ruler, she prepares her bread in summer and gathers her food in harvest" (Proverbs 6:6–8). That's the power of proverbs. They don't teach us anything new, but they do have a way with words, poking us and provoking us to look at life from another angle. In this study of the Book of Proverbs, get ready to get poked and provoked!

Pair and Share

4. Has someone ever provoked you with a proverb? What did the person say? What was the situation?

Get It Together

Lutherans memorize Luther's Small Catechism to comprehend and carry the touchstones of the Christian faith in their hearts and on their lips as they "walk in newness of life" (Romans 6:4). The six touchstones—the Six Chief Parts—are the Ten Commandments, the Creed, the Lord's Prayer, the Sacrament of Holy Baptism, the Office of the Keys and Confession, and the Sacrament of the Altar. And because the Law of God is already written on our hearts, the Ten Commandments set in stone what our hearts already know to be true, summing up the whole Law.

---

2   *Pathos* was Aristotle's favorite word for the passions accompanied by pain or pleasure.

Pair and Share

5. Ink all of the Ten Commandments in order as best you can.

Thanks to the Ten Commandments, we never have to guess what God wants us to do.[3] Commandments One through Three—sometimes called the First Table—show us how to fear, love, and trust in God above all things. Commandments Four through Ten—or the Second Table—show us how to honor, love, and cherish our neighbor as ourselves (Mark 12:30–31). Each and every action I should do keeps at least one of the Ten Commandments, and each and every action I shouldn't do breaks at least one of them. For example, when a Boy Scout helps an old lady across the street, he has kept the Fourth Commandment (Honor your father and your mother) by honoring an elder and has kept the Fifth Commandment (You shall not murder) by helping and supporting her physical need. But when the same Boy Scout looks lustfully at a young lady across the street, he has broken the Sixth Commandment (You shall not commit adultery). Thanks to the Ten Commandments, I never have to guess how to love God and my neighbor, and thanks to the Ten Commandments, I never have to guess where I have gone wrong. Every action I should do and every single sin I shouldn't do keeps or breaks one of the Ten Commandments.

Think and Ink

6. "If we say we have no sin, we deceive ourselves, and the truth is not in us" (1 John 1:8). Examine yourself. What recent sin lies heavy on your heart? Which commandment did that sin break? (Didn't I say to get ready to get poked and provoked?)

---

3   Augsburg Confession XX 1–3.

The First Step Is the Hardest

The First Commandment commands, "You shall have no other gods." *What does this mean?* We should fear, love, and trust in God above all things. Luther taught that the First Commandment is not merely the first in a list of ten; no, the First Commandment is the key to keeping all the other Commandments. Luther explains that when we keep the First Commandment first by fearing, loving, and trusting in God above all things (above all other persons, places, things, or ideas), then all the other commandments will follow on their own.[4] For example, say Tommy is tempted to puff himself up by putting his neighbor down, breaking the Eighth Commandment. If Tommy fears, loves, and trusts in God first, then he *will* keep the Eighth Commandment second. But if Tommy first fears, loves, and trusts in his namby-pamby personality more than in God, then he *will* break the Eighth Commandment second. Keep ye first the First Commandment, and all the other commandments shall be kept.

Think and Ink

7. Every single sin breaks the First Commandment first. The cause of every single sin is because we fear, love, or trust in some person, place, thing, or idea more than God. Examine the sin you noted above. How did that sin break the First Commandment first? What person, place, thing, or idea did you fear, love, or trust in more than God?

We Interrupt This Program

Here's the rub. God's Law not only shows us what we should and shouldn't do, but on top of that, it also shows us that no one has the capacity to carry it out (Romans 7:18). God's Law holds us responsible, shows us our sins, stops our mouths, declares us guilty, and justifies no one (Romans 3:19–20). What's more, not one iota, not a dot of God's Gospel is written on our hard-hearted hearts. For example, when I ask my college students to define *perfect*, they naturally answer, "Flawless, faultless, making all A's, never messing up." I tell them that Jesus says, "Be perfect, as your heavenly Father is perfect" (Matthew 5:48). They naturally think Jesus means, "Never mess up." Then, we read

---

4   Large Catechism I 48.

Matthew 5:48 in context, beginning at verse 43, and I ask them, "Now, how is your heavenly Father perfect?" Try it now for yourself—read Matthew 5:43–48.

Students are astounded. "He makes His sun rise on the evil and on the good, and sends rain on the just and on the unjust" (Matthew 5:45)—He gives grace to the ungrateful and His love to the unlovable. Our definition of perfection means "never messing up," but God's definition of perfection means "loving those who don't love you." Human beings bear the heavy log of the Law but cannot speak a speck of God's forgiving Gospel: God the Father's gracious gift of the life, death, and resurrection of His Son, Jesus Christ, for the forgiveness, life, and salvation of sinners. With His life, Jesus Christ fulfilled the Law in our place (Matthew 5:17). With His crucifixion, Jesus paid our penalty for breaking the Law in our place (Isaiah 53:4–6). With His resurrection, Jesus gives us an eternal place in heaven with Him forever (1 Corinthians 15:17–23). So like an emergency broadcast interrupting our regularly scheduled program, God graciously interrupts our broken-record breaking of His Law with the broken body and shed blood of His Son: "All have sinned and fall short of the glory of God, and are justified by His grace as a gift, through the redemption that is in Christ Jesus, whom God put forward as propitiation by His blood, to be received by faith" (Romans 3:23–25). "None is righteous, no, not one" (Romans 3:10); no one but One—just Jesus.

Yes, you and I have not feared, loved, and trusted in God above all things, but God the Father forgives, loves, and treasures you and me in His Son, Jesus Christ, first. "Almighty God in His mercy has given His Son to die for you and for His sake forgives you all your sins."[5] God the Father doesn't start anything He can't finish. It *is* finished (John 19:30)!

Motive Matters

"Since we have been justified by faith, we have peace with God" (Romans 5:1). So, since we have been justified by grace through faith for Christ's sake alone, without our works, why bother with a book of Law like Proverbs in the first place? Because when the Holy Spirit calls, gathers, and enlightens us with the Gospel, He immediately goes to work to sanctify us,[6] re-creating us in Christ Jesus for good works (Ephesians 2:8–10).[7] As the Holy Spirit calls, gathers, enlightens, and sanctifies hearts, He changes the Christian's motive for keeping the Ten Commandments from bane to blessing, from pain to pleasure (Romans 8:1–4). Lutherans divvy up three different ways the Law (the Ten

---

5   *LSB*, Confession and Absolution, page 151.
6   Solid Declaration III 41.
7   Large Catechism II 1–2.

Commandments) works within us, three different uses of the Law: first as a curb, second as a mirror, third as a guide.[8]

The First Use of the Law: You Reap What You Sow

"Trespassers will be prosecuted," cautions the first use of the Law. When the Law curbs, "No, you may not," and I cower, "I'd better not, or I'll get in trouble," then my motive for keeping the Law is the first use. Proverbs 1 curbs our bad behavior when wisdom warns we will reap what we sow (Galatians 6:7) if we refuse the reproof of the Proverbs:

> 1:24 Because I have called and you refused to listen,
>
>   have stretched out my hand and no one has heeded,
>
> 25 because you have ignored all my counsel
>
>   and would have none of my reproof,
>
> 26 I also will laugh at your calamity;
>
>   I will mock when terror strikes you,
>
> 27 when terror strikes you like a storm
>
>   and your calamity comes like a whirlwind,
>
>   when distress and anguish come upon you.
>
> 28 Then they will call upon me, but I will not answer;
>
>   they will seek me diligently but will not find me.
>
> 29 Because they hated knowledge
>
>   and did not choose the fear of the LORD,
>
> 30 would have none of my counsel
>
>   and despised all my reproof,
>
> 31 therefore they shall eat the fruit of their way,
>
>   and have their fill of their own devices.

Under the first use of the Law, I am under the provoking pressure to prove myself to God. If I "sow the wind," I will "reap the whirlwind" (Hosea 8:7).

Pair and Share

8. As you sow, so shall you reap. Think of your job or some other group you're a part of. What's a rule in that job or group that you must follow or risk being fired or removed from the group?

---

8   Solid Declaration VI 1.

The Second Use of the Law: Guilty as Sin

Mirror, mirror, on the wall, who's the vilest of them all? The second use of the Law holds a mirror up to my sins and cannot tell a lie. It declares me guilty: "Look what you've done!" In Genesis 2, God cautioned Adam and Eve with the first use of the Law: "You may surely eat of every tree of the garden, but of the tree of the knowledge of good and evil you shall not eat, for in the day that you eat of it you shall surely die" (Genesis 2:16–17). In Genesis 3, God confronts Adam and Eve with the second use of the Law:

> Because you have listened to the voice of your wife and have eaten of the tree of which I commanded you, "You shall not eat of it," cursed is the ground because of you; in pain you shall eat of it all the days of your life; thorns and thistles it shall bring forth for you; and you shall eat the plants of the field. By the sweat of your face you shall eat bread, till you return to the ground, for out of it you were taken; for you are dust, and to dust you shall return. (Genesis 3:17–19)

Adam and Eve are guilty as sin.

Our sinful nature sees sin as something silly, easy to avoid, and easy to escape if we really want to. But God sees sin as dead serious. One man's sin (the original sin of Adam) infects and defects the whole of humanity with a sinful nature and with death (Romans 5:12). Sin isn't something silly we can solve, picking and sorting the bad apples from the good apples. No, one man's sin (Adam's sin) upset the whole apple cart. One rotten apple (Adam's apple) spoiled the whole bunch. You've heard the popular proverb that the apple doesn't fall far from the tree. All of us are bad apples, fallen from Adam's apple tree. The second use of the Law holds up a mirror, shows us our sin, and rubs it in: "How do you like them apples?"

Think and Ink

9. Read Romans 5:18–19. Paul compares and contrasts Adam and Jesus. Put this passage into your own words. Sum it all up with a pithy sentence.

The Third Use of the Law: The Fruit of the Spirit

Yes, you and I are guilty as sin, but God graciously interrupts our sinful program, calling us by the Gospel. After the Holy Spirit calls, gathers, and enlightens us with God the Father's forgiveness and grace in His Son, Jesus Christ, then the Holy Spirit sanctifies us to see the Law in a new light: as a guide, the third use of the Law.[9] Since there is now "no condemnation for those who are in Christ Jesus" (Romans 8:1), the Law not only shows us the forbidden fruit we shouldn't eat; the Holy Spirit now also produces in us the fruit that is replete with His love that fulfills the Law (Romans 8:4; 13:10). Through the Gospel, the Holy Spirit frees us from the provoking pressure to prove how good we are to God to God producing His Christ-created fruit in us—from the pressures of the first and second uses of the Law to seeing the Law, as free people, in its third use.

Imagine Tommy getting Tammy flowers, chocolate, and a candlelit dinner for Valentine's Day. What if Tommy said to himself, "If I don't get these gifts for Tammy, she'll break up with me"? Tommy's motive would be the first use of the Law. What if Tammy said, "You didn't get me anything for Valentine's? You're in big trouble, Tommy!" If he then goes and gets gifts, Tommy's motive is the second use of the Law. But if Tommy goes and gets gifts ahead of time not because he has to but because Tammy loves him, then Tommy's gifts are no longer forced and fettered exasperations of the first and second uses of the Law but gifts given from a free and cheerful spirit. It's obvious which scenario is best.

That's Tommy and Tammy, but now imagine you and God. If I grudgingly ask, "Do I *have* to love God?" then my motive is the first use of the Law. If I grovelingly ask, "How will I make up for my sins?" then my motive is the second use of the Law. But when God the Father forgives, loves, and treasures you in the life, death, and resurrection of His Son first and the Holy Spirit produces in you the fruit of fear, love, and trust in God, then you know the Law in its third use and your motive is the Gospel. How can I fear, love, and trust in God above all things? The Holy Spirit answers with the good ole Ten Commandments:[10] "Your heavenly Father loves it when you honor your father and mother (the Fourth Commandment). He loves it when you help and support your neighbor in every physical need (the Fifth Commandment)." Amazed, we reply, "He does?!" "He sure does," responds the Holy Spirit. And the Holy Spirit reminds us of the Gospel again (John 15:26): "First things first, you can fear,

---

9   Solid Declaration VI 4–5, 11, 17.
10   Augsburg Confession XX 1–3.

love, and trust in God above all things (the First Commandment) because He forgives, loves, and treasures you with the Gospel first" (see 1 John 4:19). More than Tammy loves flowers and chocolate, God loves it when we keep the Ten Commandments because He forgives, loves, and treasures us with the Gospel first. Motive matters to God and you.

Hence, through the Gospel, the Holy Spirit frees us from the provoking pressure to prove how good we are to God to God producing His Christ-created fruit in us—from the first and second uses of the Law to the third use (Colossians 3:17). The Gospel transforms the Ten Commandments from a list of no-nos and dos and don'ts to a list of love languages for God and for our neighbor. Thanks to the Ten Commandments, we never have to guess how to love God and our neighbor best. Under the Gospel, Christians fear, love, and trust in God above all things *second* because God forgives, loves, and treasures us *first*.

Think and Ink

10. "Whatever you do, in word or deed, do everything in the name of the Lord Jesus, giving thanks to God the Father through Him" (Colossians 3:17). What's one deed you need to do today? What would it be like if your motive for doing that good work wasn't just the pressure to prove yourself to God or someone else (the first use of the Law), or because you felt guilty for something you did and were trying to make up for it (the second use of the Law), but because you fear, love, and trust in God because He forgives, loves, and treasures you first (the Gospel)? God the Father forgives, loves, and treasures you in Christ Jesus *first*!

Mixed Motives

I wish I was always motivated by the Gospel and led by the Spirit and knew the Law only in its third use. But nothing I do is as pure in motivation and execution as I wish it were. I wish I was always motivated by the Gospel for my Monday morning 8:00 a.m. class, praying, "I thank You, my heavenly Father, through Jesus Christ, Your dear Son, that You have kept me this night from all harm and danger. I can't wait for the Holy Spirit to show Your wisdom and love to these students through me!" But honestly, sometimes I don't feel like that, and I must be curbed by the first use of the Law: "Either get up, shape up, and teach that 8:00 a.m. class, or ship out!" my provost provokes.[11]

The good news is that Lutherans are not ethical idealists;[12] Lutherans are a mixed bag of motives. The apostle Paul knows what I'm going through. Paul called it like it is and confessed, "I have the desire to do what is right, but not the ability to carry it out. For I do not do the good I want, but the evil I do not want is what I keep on doing" (Romans 7:18–19). Jesus confirms our fallen nature: "The spirit indeed is willing, but the flesh is weak" (Matthew 26:41). With Jesus and Paul, Lutherans lay their cards on the table and confess the albatross around their necks, confessing with Luther in Latin, "We are *simul iustus et peccator*"—simultaneously saint and sinner.[13] This paradox is simultaneously both bane and blessing, pain and pleasure, keeping us honest and keeping us dependent upon the Holy Spirit (Romans 8:14–15). I am perfectly justified—just as if I'd never sinned—because of Jesus. At the same time, I can honestly confess that my best efforts still suffer from the imperfections of my sinful nature. Americans love the Declaration of Independence, but Lutherans love the declaration of their dependence on the Holy Spirit: "I believe that I cannot by my own reason or strength believe in Jesus Christ, my Lord, or come to Him; but the Holy Spirit has called me by the Gospel, enlightened me with His gifts, sanctified and kept me in the true faith."[14] The Marines are *semper fidelis*—always faithful. The Coast Guard is *semper paratus*—always ready. Until we die, Lutherans are *semper simul iustus et peccator*—always simultaneously saint and sinner.[15]

Pair and Share

11. Lutherans are *semper simul iustus et peccator*. Examine a good work you did this past week. What was your motive? Was it the first use of

---

11   Epitome VI 5–6.
12   Epitome II 7, 12.
13   Epitome VI 3–4.
14   Small Catechism, Third Article.
15   Large Catechism II 57–58.

the Law—you felt pressured to prove yourself to God or someone else? Was it the second use of the Law—you felt guilty for something you did and were trying to make up for it? Or was it the Gospel—you feared, loved, and trusted in God because you are forgiven, loved, and treasured by God? Or was it a mixture of all three?

Out with the Bad, In with the Good

Pair and Share

12. What comes to mind when you think of Baptism?

Think and Ink

13. Read Romans 6:1–11. How does Paul describe Baptism? Put it in your own words.

Since I'm *semper simul* saint and sinner, I can just keep on sinning, right? God will keep forgiving! Paul snorts and retorts in Greek, "*Me genoito*," "No way. Uh-uh. Forget it!" Then Paul reminds us to remember our Baptism: "How can we who died to sin still live in it?" (Romans 6:2). "I've died to sin? When did that happen?" I ask. "When you were baptized!" says Paul. "All of us who have been baptized into Christ Jesus were baptized into His death. We were buried therefore with Him by baptism into death, in order that, just as Christ was raised from the dead by the glory of the Father, we too might walk in newness of life" (Romans 6:3–4). Here, he reminds us that Baptism is not only the beginning of Christian life (Matthew 28:19–20); Baptism is also the daily battle of Christian life. Luther puts it this way: Baptism "indicates that the Old Adam in us"—our sinful nature—"should by daily contrition and repentance be drowned and die with all sins and evil desires, and that a new man should daily emerge and arise to live before God in righteousness and purity forever."[16]

There are only two words you need to remember about Baptism. They're easy to remember because they both start with B, as in *Baptism*, and they both have only four letters, three of which are the same. The two words are *bury* and *buoy*. Baptism buries our sins in the crucifixion of Jesus, and Baptism buoys our lives in the resurrection of Jesus. Baptism buries the bad and buoys the good. Whenever I babble and bubble, "Can I keep on sinning? God'll keep forgiving" (Romans 6:1), that's the time to engage in the battle of Baptism, burying the old, sinful nature in me and buoying the new creation in me (Romans 6:2–4). As a baptized Christian, you never fight this battle alone. Baptism gives the gift of the Holy Spirit (Acts 2:38), and now the same Holy Spirit who raised Jesus from the dead lives in you (Romans 8:11).

Paul says, "The death He died He died to sin, once for all, but the life He lives He lives to God" (Romans 6:10). Because Baptism buries us in the crucifixion of Jesus and buoys us in the resurrection of Jesus, Paul says you have the right to "consider yourselves dead to sin and alive to God in Christ Jesus" (Romans 6:11). Since we are *semper simul* saint and sinner, Lutherans remember their Baptism every day, burying the sinner and buoying the saint with the help of the Holy Spirit in the daily battle of Baptism.

I Won't Take No for an Answer

Why study a provoking book of Law like the Book of Proverbs? Because you are baptized! Yes, we confess we are *semper simul* saint and sinner. Yes, we confess we are a mixed bag of motives. Yes, we confess our sinful nature needs a daily burial in Baptism. But buried in the crucifixion of Jesus and buoyed in the resurrection of Jesus, you *are* dead to sin and alive to God in Christ Jesus. Because we are forgiven, loved, and treasured children of God, the Holy Spirit makes our bodies His temple (1 Corinthians 6:19–20) and sanctifies our motives for keeping the Law from the pressure to prove ourselves to God to God producing His Christ-created fruit in us (Ephesians 2:10). Baptized into Christ and created in Christ, Christians are empowered by the Holy Spirit (Romans 8:14) to fear, love, and trust in God above all things because God forgives, loves, and treasures them first (1 John 4:19).[17]

---

16   Small Catechism, Baptism, Fourth Part.
17   Epitome II 15, 17.

All Good Things Come in Threes

How will we study the Book of Proverbs? As my momma used to say, "There's more than one way to skin a cat." We'll skin the cat in this way, under these three headings: Analyze, Personalize, and Memorize.

Analyze: Work Smarter, Not Harder

First, this study categorizes the proverbs of the Book of Proverbs according to the Ten Commandments. As we noted, the Ten Commandments sum up the whole Law. Each and every action I should do and every single sin I shouldn't do keeps or breaks one of the Ten Commandments, and every single sin breaks the First Commandment first. Since the Book of Proverbs is a book of Law, this study has categorized almost all of the proverbs according to the commandment that proverb speaks of keeping or breaking. If you've read through Proverbs before, you've noticed that the proverbs often change subjects from verse to verse at random. For example, Proverbs 10:1 ("A wise son makes a glad father, but a foolish son is a sorrow to his mother") is a Fourth Commandment proverb. Proverbs 10:2 ("Treasures gained by wickedness do not profit, but righteousness delivers from death") is a Seventh Commandment proverb. Proverbs 10:3 ("The LORD does not let the righteous go hungry, but He thwarts the craving of the wicked") is a Ninth Commandment proverb. This fluidity can make reading the Book of Proverbs like reaching into a jar full of fortune cookies—you never know what you're going to get. Instead of rambling at random, this study categorizes all of the First Commandment proverbs together, all the Second Commandment proverbs together, all the Third Commandment proverbs together, and so on. Each chapter deals with one of the Ten Commandments. In each chapter, you'll analyze all the proverbs for just one commandment at a time, allowing you to work smarter, not harder.

Personalize: The Best Is Yet to Come

Second, you'll personalize your favorite proverb for each of the Ten Commandments. We all have our favorite popular proverbs we like to say: "Absence makes the heart grow fonder," "Actions speak louder than words," "All's well that ends well." Won't it be fun to have ten more proverbs in your repertoire that are not just popular, pithy statements but are also the powerful Word of God (2 Timothy 3:16)? At the end of each chapter, you'll choose your personal favorite proverb for that chapter's commandment. At the end of this study, you'll have your top ten proverbs from the Book of Proverbs, one for each of the Ten Commandments. The best is yet to come!

Memorize: You Can Say That Again

Third, you'll memorize your ten favorite proverbs for each commandment. Many of us memorized Luther's Small Catechism in confirmation to carry the touchstones of the Christian faith in our heads and hearts so that we can exercise that faith with our lips and hands. Not everyone likes to memorize anymore, but, terse and mesmerizing, proverbs are meant to be memorized. We memorize proverbs today to utilize them tomorrow. Whether the Holy Spirit provokes you to utter one out loud to others or to say one silently to yourself (John 14:26), all of us need to be poked and provoked by the sharp, double-edged sword of God's Word (Hebrews 4:12). The Book of Proverbs has thirty-one chapters with twenty to thirty-five proverbs per chapter. In this study, you'll analyze almost all of them, personalize your favorites, and memorize only your top ten. Take this time to re-memorize Luther's explanations of the Ten Commandments from the Small Catechism too. To jog your memory for years to come, ink your favorite proverb for each commandment on the Summary Sheet in the back of the book. At the end of the study, tear it out, tape it in your Bible, and tack it to your heart. That way, you're *semper paratus* to *carpe diem*—always ready to utilize God's wisdom on your neighbor and yourself today and tomorrow.

The key passage for this study is Proverbs 22:17–18:

> Incline your ear, and hear the words of the wise,
>> and apply your heart to my knowledge,
> for it will be pleasant if you keep them within you,
>> if all of them are ready on your lips.

This study will either be quality time or a waste of time. This study won't be a waste of time and "will be pleasant if you keep" your top ten proverbs "within you, if all of them are ready on your lips." You can say that again.

Take It or Leave It

This Bible study categorizes the proverbs of the Book of Proverbs according to the Ten Commandments so that you can easily analyze, personalize, and memorize your top ten favorite proverbs from the Book of Proverbs, one for each of the Ten Commandments, provoking you to fear, love, and trust in God above all things because God forgives, loves, and treasures you first (1 John 4:19). Get ready to get poked and provoked by *Provoking Proverbs*!

Think and Ink

14. Review the preface and ink the top three points you learned today.

Merciful Father, through Holy Baptism You called us to be Your own possession. Grant that our lives may evidence the working of Your Holy Spirit in love, joy, peace, patience, kindness, goodness, faithfulness, gentleness, and self-control, according to the image of Your only-begotten Son, Jesus Christ, our Savior. Amen.[18]

---

18   *LSB*, "Life as a baptized child of God," page 310.

CHAPTER 1

THE FIRST COMMANDMENT

You shall have no other gods. *What does this mean?* We should fear, love, and trust in God above all things.

Deep Memory

Dig deep and ink the top three points you learned from the preface.

You Shall Have No Other Gods

What does it mean to have a god? Luther taught that everyone makes a god out of what their heart most desires:

> For example, the heathen who put their trust in power and dominion elevated Jupiter as the supreme god. Others, who were bent on riches, happiness, or pleasure, and a life of ease, elevated Hercules, Mercury [gods of wealth and prosperity], Venus [the goddess of love], or other gods. Pregnant women elevated Diana or Lucina, and so on.[1]

What does it mean, then, "to have a god"? Luther answers:

> A god means that from which we are to expect all good and in which we are to take refuge in all distress. So, to have a God is nothing other than trusting and believing Him with the heart. I have often said that the confidence and faith of the heart alone make both God and an idol. If your faith and trust is right, then your god is also true. On the other hand, if your trust is false and wrong, then you do not have the

---

1   Large Catechism I 18. Brackets added.

true God. . . . Now, I say that whatever you set your heart on and put your trust in is truly your god.[2]

Pair and Share

1. What does it mean to have a god? Put Luther's words in your own words. Sum it all up with a pithy sentence.

Think and Ink

2. Think of three things (a person, place, thing, or idea) that you are often tempted to fear, love, or trust in more than God. "These are your gods" (Exodus 32:4). When you identify your own false gods, then the First Commandment starts to hit home.

A Good Beginning Is Half the Battle

We should fear, love, and trust in God above all things. Solomon sets a firm foundation with his very first proverb: "The fear of the LORD is the beginning of knowledge" (Proverbs 1:7).

1:7 The fear of the LORD is the beginning of knowledge;

fools despise wisdom and instruction.

8:13 The fear of the LORD is hatred of evil.

Pride and arrogance and the way of evil

and perverted speech I hate.

9:10 The fear of the LORD is the beginning of wisdom,

and the knowledge of the Holy One is insight.

2   Large Catechism I 2–3.

14:2 Whoever walks in uprightness fears the LORD,

but he who is devious in his ways despises Him.

15:33 The fear of the LORD is instruction in wisdom,

and humility comes before honor.

31:30 Charm is deceitful, and beauty is vain,

but a woman who fears the LORD is to be praised.

Mark and Remark

Mark your favorite proverb above and remark why you chose it.

Better Safe Than Sorry

"The fear of the LORD is the beginning of knowledge" (Proverbs 1:7). Really? Doesn't the fear of the Lord just mean reverence and respect? Well, that's one side of the coin. Certainly, we revere and respect God the Father, Son, and Holy Spirit—our Creator, Redeemer, and Sanctifier. On this side of the coin, God is awesome. On the other side of the coin, God is also awful—He is our judge! With the First Commandment, God curbs and cautions us with awful fear: "I the LORD your God am a jealous God, visiting the iniquity of the fathers on the children to the third and fourth generation of those who hate Me" (Exodus 20:5). God is not afraid to use fear to help free us from the false gods we fear, love, and trust more than Him.

Pair and Share

3. Why did you need to have a healthy fear of your parents and teachers growing up? If you have children, why do your kids need to have a healthy fear of you?

Pair and Share

4. Read Deuteronomy 5:22–29. When God gave the Ten Commandments to the Israelites in the Old Testament, He scared the living daylights out of them. Was God glad or sad about this? Why?

Worldly wisdom tells us, "Better safe than sorry," meaning that it's better to be on the safe side than the sorry side. Proverbs tells us that the fear of the Lord is the safe side. Choose sides.

3:7 Be not wise in your own eyes;

fear the LORD, and turn away from evil.

8 It will be healing to your flesh

and refreshment to your bones.

3:25 Do not be afraid of sudden terror

or of the ruin of the wicked, when it comes,

26 for the LORD will be your confidence

and will keep your foot from being caught.

10:27 The fear of the LORD prolongs life,

but the years of the wicked will be short.

14:26 In the fear of the LORD one has strong confidence,

and his children will have a refuge.

27 The fear of the LORD is a fountain of life,

that one may turn away from the snares of death.

15:16 Better is a little with the fear of the LORD

than great treasure and trouble with it.

19:23 The fear of the LORD leads to life,

and whoever has it rests satisfied;

he will not be visited by harm.[3]

---

3   There are always exceptions to general rules. When Christians suffer, it always works together for good (Romans 8:28). Luther counsels, "Just do what is your duty. Let God manage how He will support you and provide enough for you" (Large Catechism I 165).

23:17 Let not your heart envy sinners,

>but continue in the fear of the LORD all the day.

28:14 Blessed is the one who fears the LORD always,

>but whoever hardens his heart will fall into calamity.

29:25 The fear of man lays a snare,

>but whoever trusts in the LORD is safe.

Mark and Remark

Mark your favorite proverb above and remark why you chose it.

Pride Goes before a Fall

Did you ever play king of the mountain when you were little? It's not a game for the weak and meek. In the Sermon on the Mount, *the* King of the Mountain depicts a paradoxical path to the top: "Blessed are the meek" (Matthew 5:5). To get to the top, humility fears, loves, and trusts in God above all things because God forgives, loves, and treasures you first. But before a fall, pride plays first fiddle and forgets God—fearing, loving, and trusting in itself above all things. To take us to the top, "God opposes the proud but gives grace to the humble" (James 4:6). "Whoever exalts himself will be humbled, and whoever humbles himself will be exalted" (Matthew 23:12). "Humble yourselves, therefore, under the mighty hand of God so that at the proper time He may exalt you" (1 Peter 5:6).

11:2 When pride comes, then comes disgrace,

>but with the humble is wisdom.

15:25 The LORD tears down the house of the proud

>but maintains the widow's boundaries.

16:5 Everyone who is arrogant in heart is an abomination to the LORD;

>be assured, he will not go unpunished.

16:18 Pride goes before destruction,

and a haughty spirit before a fall.

18:12 Before destruction a man's heart is haughty,

but humility comes before honor.

21:4 Haughty eyes and a proud heart,

the lamp of the wicked, are sin.

25:27 It is not good to eat much honey,

nor is it glorious to seek one's own glory.

26:12 Do you see a man who is wise in his own eyes?

There is more hope for a fool than for him.

29:23 One's pride will bring him low,

but he who is lowly in spirit will obtain honor.

Mark and Remark

Mark your favorite proverb above and remark why you chose it.

Warts and All

The warty, pimply lord protector of England, Oliver Cromwell (1599–1658), asked artist Peter Lely to paint his portrait exactly as he saw him, "warts and all." Today, when you love someone "warts and all," you see both the good and the bad and love him or her unconditionally. God is omniscient: He knows and names all the stars (Psalm 147:4–5) and knows and numbers all the hairs on your head (Matthew 10:29–31). "Where shall I go from Your Spirit? Or where shall I flee from Your presence?" the psalmist asks (Psalm 139:7). Nothing escapes the eagle eyes of God. He sees everything about you—inside and out, sins and sorrows, warts and all. And He won't let the warts hinder or hamper His unconditional love for you in His Son (1 John 4:10).

5:21 A man's ways are before the eyes of the LORD,
and He ponders all his paths.

15:3 The eyes of the LORD are in every place,
keeping watch on the evil and the good.

15:11 Sheol and Abaddon lie open before the LORD;
how much more the hearts of the children of man![4]

16:2 All the ways of a man are pure in his own eyes,
but the LORD weighs the spirit.

17:3 The crucible is for silver, and the furnace is for gold,
and the LORD tests hearts.

20:12 The hearing ear and the seeing eye,
the LORD has made them both.

20:27 The spirit of man is the lamp of the LORD,
searching all his innermost parts.

21:2 Every way of a man is right in his own eyes,
but the LORD weighs the heart.

22:12 The eyes of the LORD keep watch over knowledge,
but He overthrows the words of the traitor.

29:13 The poor man and the oppressor meet together;
the LORD gives light to the eyes of both.

30:4 Who has ascended to heaven and come down?
Who has gathered the wind in His fists?
Who has wrapped up the waters in a garment?
Who has established all the ends of the earth?
What is His name, and what is His Son's name?
Surely you know!

---

4   *Sheol* and *Abaddon* are Old Testament names for the "hereafter"—the realm of the dead who have departed this life.

Mark and Remark

Mark your favorite proverb above and remark why you chose it.

Man Proposes, God Disposes

We don't use the word *penultimate* much, but we should. *Penultimate* means "next to the last"—not the ultimate, but next to the ultimate. Zechariah is the penultimate book of the Old Testament, but Malachi is the ultimate. Jude is the penultimate in the New Testament, but Revelation is the ultimate. The vice president of the United States is penultimate, but the buck stops with the president. God is ultimate, but God has given humans a penultimate part to play: "Let us make man in Our image, after Our likeness. And let them have dominion over the fish of the sea and over the birds of the heavens and over the livestock and over all the earth and over every creeping thing that creeps on the earth" (Genesis 1:26).

Since you are made in the image of God, you have a penultimate part to play—to have dominion with the *Dominus*. "Have dominion" in Genesis 1:26 comes from the ancient scholar Jerome's Latin "*dominamini*" in the Vulgate version of the Bible. Each time Jerome came across the Tetragrammaton, YHWH, the four-letter Hebrew name for God, he translated it "*Dominus*"—Latin for "Lord."[5] Made in the image of the *Dominus*, your role is to have dominion with the *Dominus*—to have dominion over creation with the Creator. To "have dominion" doesn't mean to have our way with the world however we please. No, to "have dominion" means to mirror the way the *Dominus* has dominion. How does He have dominion? He has eternal care and concern for His creation (Romans 8:18–25). He looks after life on His earth (Matthew 6:25–33). He creates a place for everything and places everything in its place. When you and I express God's kind of ethical care and concern for His creation, that's having dominion with the *Dominus*.

Ultimately, He's got the whole world in His hands, but penultimately, God has given us a part to play. Exercising dominion, we make plans to help the world work as effectively and efficiently as possible. Farmers farm the land.

---

5   Modern English Bibles mark this by writing "LORD" in small capital letters.

Students study for exams. Nurses nurse patients back to health. But our plans, no matter how well planned, do not always go according to plan. The old adage "Man proposes, God disposes" means that our plans are penultimate; God's plans are ultimate.

> Come now, you who say, "Today or tomorrow we will go into such and such a town and spend a year there and trade and make profit."—yet you do not know what tomorrow will bring. What is your life? For you are a mist that appears for a little time and then vanishes. Instead you ought to say, "If the Lord wills, we will live and do this or that." (James 4:13–15)

No matter how much control we covet, Proverbs propounds that we should fear, love, and trust in God above all things first.

3:5 Trust in the LORD with all your heart,

and do not lean on your own understanding.

6 In all your ways acknowledge Him,

and He will make straight your paths.

14:12 There is a way that seems right to a man,

but its end is the way to death.

16:1 The plans of the heart belong to man,

but the answer of the tongue is from the LORD.

16:9 The heart of man plans his way,

but the LORD establishes his steps.

16:20 Whoever gives thought to the word will discover good,

and blessed is he who trusts in the LORD.[6]

16:33 The lot is cast into the lap,

but its every decision is from the LORD.

19:21 Many are the plans in the mind of a man,

But it is the purpose of the LORD that will stand.

20:24 A man's steps are from the LORD;

how then can man understand his way?

---

6   *Small Catechism*, First Petition: "God's name is kept holy when the Word of God is taught in its truth and purity, and we, as the children of God, also lead holy lives according to it."

21:1 The king's heart is a stream of water in the hand of the LORD;

He turns it wherever He will.

21:30 No wisdom, no understanding, no counsel

can avail against the LORD.

31 The horse is made ready for the day of battle,

But the victory belongs to the LORD.

27:1 Do not boast about tomorrow,

for you do not know what a day may bring.

29:26 Many seek the face of a ruler,

but it is from the LORD that a man gets justice.

Mark and Remark

Mark your favorite proverb above and remark why you chose it.

First Things First

Let's use the word *penultimate* some more. As we noted in the preface, Luther taught that the First Commandment is not merely the first in a list; the First Commandment is the key to keeping all the other commandments: "Where the heart is rightly set toward God . . . and this commandment is observed, all the other commandments follow."[7] Luther explains that when we keep the First Commandment first by fearing, loving, and trusting in God above all things (above all other persons, places, things, or ideas), then all the other commandments will follow on their own, second. In other words, Commandments Two through Ten are penultimate, but the First Commandment is ultimate. When Tommy looks at and lusts after a woman other than his wife, he has penultimately broken the Sixth Commandment, but he has ultimately broken the First Commandment, fearing, loving, and trusting in the image of another woman more than God. When Tammy gossips about a co-worker and hurts his reputation, she has penultimately broken the Eighth Commandment, but she has ultimately broken the First Commandment, fearing, loving,

---

7   Large Catechism I 48.

and trusting in puffing herself up by putting others down more than God. First things first: keep the First Commandment first, and all the other commandments will be kept second.

Think and Ink

5. What recent sin lies heavy on your heart? Which of Commandments Two through Ten did that sin break? How did that sin break the First Commandment first? What person, place, thing, or idea did you fear, love, or trust more than God?

Don't Put the Cart before the Horse

To conclude, let's use the word *penultimate* one more time. Yes, Commandments Two through Ten are penultimate to the ultimate First Commandment: we should fear, love, and trust in God above all things. But even the First Commandment is penultimate to God's ultimate message of the Gospel: God the Father, Son, and Holy Spirit forgives, loves, and treasures you first. God forgives us not because we fear, love, and trust in Him first; no, God forgave us while we were still sinners (Romans 5:8) first. God so loved the world that He gave His only-begotten Son while we were still unlovable (John 3:16) first. Whenever you feel the pressure to keep the First Commandment, fearing, loving, and trusting in God above all things, don't put the cart before the horse. God the Father, Son, and Holy Spirit forgives, loves, and treasures you first.

Personalize and Memorize

"We should fear, love, and trust in God above all things." With the Holy Spirit's help (John 14:26; Romans 8:11), keeping the First Commandment means holding fast to the Gospel first. Holding fast to the Gospel, analyze all the First Commandment proverbs you previously marked and choose your favorite. Which proverb will help you keep the First Commandment with fear, love, and trust because you are baptized—because you are created in Christ—because God the Father forgives, loves, and treasures you in His Son first? Memorize it. Imagine a moment this week when you'll utilize your proverb. It will be pleasant if you keep it within you, if it is always ready on your lips (Proverbs 22:18).

Lord God, author and source of all that is good, give us wisdom to fear Your wrath, strength to love You above all things, and faith to trust in Your promises alone, that by Your grace we may serve You all our days and finally come to inherit Your heavenly kingdom; through Jesus Christ, Your Son, our Lord, who lives and reigns with You and the Holy Spirit, one God, now and forever. Amen.[8]

---

8   *Luther's Small Catechism with Explanation*, First Commandment, prayer.

39

THE SECOND COMMANDMENT

You shall not misuse the name of the LORD your God. *What does this mean?* We should fear and love God so that we do not curse, swear, use satanic arts, lie, or deceive by His name, but call upon it in every trouble, pray, praise, and give thanks.

Deep Memory

Dig deep and ink your First Commandment proverb.

You Shall Not Misuse the Name

Because God forgives, loves, and treasures us first, we should fear, love, and trust in God above all things, keeping the First Commandment. Because God forgives, loves, and treasures us first, we should fear, love, and trust in God with our lips second, keeping the Second Commandment. For Luther, keeping the Second Commandment is the same thing as the practice of prayer:

> The first thing to know is that it is our duty to pray because of God's commandment. For that's what we heard in the Second Commandment, "You shall not take the name of the LORD your God in vain" [Exodus 20:7]. We are required to praise that holy name and call upon it in every need, or to pray. To call upon God's name is nothing other than to pray. . . . Prayer is just as strictly and seriously commanded as all other commandments: to have no other God, not to kill, not to steal,

and so on. Let no one think that it makes no difference whether he prays or not.[1]

While just as important as all the other commandments, the Book of Proverbs does not provide a profusion of proverbs on prayer and keeping the Second Commandment. However, here is what Proverbs does have to say about this commandment.

A Good Name Is Better Than Precious Ointment

A name is a word by which a person, place, thing, or idea is identified. Most names have etymological meanings.

Pair and Share

1. What does your name mean? Google it. Does your name match your personality?

Christians keep the Second Commandment "in the name of Jesus." The name of Jesus is the name above all names (Philippians 2:9–11), and to pray "in the name of Jesus" (Colossians 3:17) means to pray under His saving identity, authority, protection, and reputation.

Pair and Share

2. Read Exodus 3:14 and Matthew 1:21. What do the names YHWH and Jesus mean?

"Dragging someone's name through the mud" means ruining their reputation. "A good name is better than precious ointment" (Ecclesiastes 7:1) because having a good name means having a good reputation. There's a reason no one names their sons Judas, Benedict, and Adolf anymore. What's in a name? A lot!

---

1   Large Catechism III 5–6. Brackets in original.

10:7 The memory of the righteous is a blessing,

      but the name of the wicked will rot.

22:1 A good name is to be chosen rather than great riches,

      and favor is better than silver or gold.

Mark and Remark

Mark your favorite proverb above and remark why you chose it.

It's What's Inside That Counts

"Never judge a book by its cover" because "appearances are deceiving." Because all of us are guilty of breaking the First Commandment on the inside first, none of us can keep the Second Commandment on the outside second. But because Christ has drawn near to us first, we can "with confidence draw near to the throne of grace, that we may receive mercy and find grace to help in time of need" (Hebrews 4:16) second.

15:8 The sacrifice of the wicked is an abomination to the LORD,

      but the prayer of the upright is acceptable to Him.

15:29 The LORD is far from the wicked,

      but He hears the prayer of the righteous.

19:3 When a man's folly brings his way to ruin,

      his heart rages against the LORD.

28:9 If one turns away his ear from hearing the law,

      even his prayer is an abomination.

28:13 Whoever conceals his transgressions will not prosper,

      but he who confesses and forsakes them will obtain mercy.

Mark and Remark

Mark your favorite proverb above and remark why you chose it.

In God We Trust

How can a country that guarantees the freedom of religion have "In God We Trust" for its official motto? Groups have debated both sides of this coin ever since its 1956 adoption. For the sake of peace, God has instituted two kingdoms on earth.[2] The left-hand kingdom is the secular kingdom that restrains wickedness with the sword of the government (Romans 13:1–7). The right-hand kingdom is the spiritual kingdom through which the Holy Spirit creates Christians with the words of the Gospel (Colossians 1:13–14). Christians are citizens of both kingdoms. On one hand, we'll be wringing our hands over "In God We Trust" for decades to come in the left-hand kingdom. On the other hand, "In God We Trust" fits in the right-hand kingdom like a glove. When we fear, love, and trust in God above all things, keeping the First Commandment, then we can call upon Him in every trouble, pray, praise, and give thanks, keeping the Second Commandment.

16:3 Commit your work to the LORD,

and your plans will be established.

18:10 The name of the LORD is a strong tower;

the righteous man runs into it and is safe.

30:5 Every word of God proves true;

He is a shield to those who take refuge in Him.

6 Do not add to His words,

lest He rebuke you and you be found a liar.

---

2   See *On Temporal Authority, Luther's Works:* American Edition, volume 45 (Philadelphia: Fortress Press, 1962), pages 75–129.

Mark and Remark

Mark your favorite proverb above and remark why you chose it.

Personalize and Memorize

"Call upon [Him] in every trouble, pray, praise, and give thanks." With the Holy Spirit's help (John 14:26; Romans 8:11), keeping the Second Commandment means drawing near to the One who draws near to you first (Hebrews 4:15–16). Analyze all the Second Commandment proverbs you marked and choose your favorite. Which proverb will help you keep the Second Commandment with fear, love, and trust because you are baptized—because you are created in Christ—because God the Father forgives, loves, and treasures you in His Son first? Memorize it. Imagine a moment this week when you'll utilize your proverb. It will be pleasant if you keep it within you, if it is always ready on your lips (Proverbs 22:18).

Holy Father, purify our lips from every misuse of Your name by cursing, swearing, superstition, lying, or deception. Open our mouths to reverence Your holy name, calling upon it in every time of trouble, praying for what You promise to give, praising You for Your glory, and giving thanks to You as the giver of every good and perfect gift; this we ask in the name that gives us access to You, the name of Jesus Christ, our Lord. Amen.[3]

---

3   *Luther's Small Catechism with Explanation*, Second Commandment, prayer.

CHAPTER 3

THE THIRD COMMANDMENT

Remember the Sabbath day by keeping it holy. *What does this mean?* We should fear and love God so that we do not despise preaching and His Word, but hold it sacred and gladly hear and learn it.

Deep Memory

Dig deep and ink your First and Second Commandment proverbs.

Remember the Sabbath

If keeping the First Commandment is fearing, loving, and trusting in God with your heart, and keeping the Second Commandment is fearing, loving, and trusting in God with your lips, then keeping the Third Commandment is fearing, loving, and trusting in God with your ears. Luther teaches that the Third Commandment is a gift of time given by God (1) for rest and refreshment after a week of work and (2) for hearing and learning God's Word.[1] In this chapter, we'll learn that the Third Commandment pairs labor with leisure, vocation with vacation, and responsibility with recreation. God wants us to work hard and play hard. Before we focus on working hard, let us first focus on playing hard. Keeping the Third Commandment first means resting from our God-given vocations to take a vacation with the Word of God, giving it quality time to "pass from the ear to the heart, from the heart to lip, and from the lip to the life."[2]

---

1   Large Catechism I 83–84.
2   *LSB*, Prayers for Worship, "For blessing on the Word."

2:1 My son, if you receive My words

and treasure up My commandments with you,

2 making your ear attentive to wisdom

and inclining your heart to understanding;

3 yes, if you call out for insight

and raise your voice for understanding,

4 if you seek it like silver

and search for it as for hidden treasures,

5 then you will understand the fear of the LORD

and find the knowledge of God.

6 For the LORD gives wisdom;

from His mouth come knowledge and understanding;

7 He stores up sound wisdom for the upright;

He is a shield to those who walk in integrity,

8 guarding the paths of justice

and watching over the way of His saints.

9 Then you will understand righteousness and justice

and equity, every good path;

10 for wisdom will come into your heart,

and knowledge will be pleasant to your soul;

11 discretion will watch over you,

understanding will guard you,

12 delivering you from the way of evil,

from men of perverted speech,

13 who forsake the paths of uprightness

to walk in the ways of darkness,

14 who rejoice in doing evil

and delight in the perverseness of evil,

15 men whose paths are crooked,

and who are devious in their ways.

Mark and Remark

Mark your favorite proverb above and remark why you chose it.

In the Beginning Was the Word

Words and wisdom go together. On an exam, if I ask my students to give me their wisdom and they give me no words, then I give them a letter—an *F*. Words and wisdom go together. Scripture says that words and wisdom always go together with one more thing: Jesus Christ. Jesus Christ, the eternally begotten Second Person of the Trinity, *is* the Word and wisdom of God: "In the beginning was the Word, and the Word was with God, and the Word was God. He was in the beginning with God" (John 1:1–2). Through Jesus Christ, the Word and wisdom of God, creation was created: "All things were made through Him, and without Him was not any thing made that was made" (John 1:3). And through Jesus Christ, the Word and wisdom of God, creation is re-created: "Whoever hears My word and believes Him who sent Me has eternal life" (John 5:24). When many of Jesus' disciples turned and walked away from Him, Jesus asked the twelve, "'Do you want to go away as well?' Simon Peter answered, 'Lord to whom shall we go? You have the words of eternal life'" (John 6:67–68). Words and wisdom *and* Jesus Christ always go together. Proverbs 8 proffers what Christians know to be true: wisdom is not merely an abstract idea like physics or philosophy; wisdom is a concrete person: "The Word became flesh and dwelt among us" (John 1:14). When the Holy Spirit helps you keep the Third Commandment, seeking wisdom in the Word of God, you are seeking Jesus Christ Himself (John 5:39; 15:26).

8:22 "The LORD possessed Me at the beginning of His work,
    the first of His acts of old.
23 Ages ago I was set up,
    at the first, before the beginning of the earth.
24 When there were no depths I was brought forth,
    when there were no springs abounding with water.
25 Before the mountains had been shaped,
    before the hills, I was brought forth,
26 before He had made the earth with its fields,
    or the first of the dust of the world.
27 When He established the heavens, I was there;
    when He drew a circle on the face of the deep,
28 when He made firm the skies above,
    when He established the fountains of the deep,
29 when He assigned to the sea its limit,
    so that the waters might not transgress His command,

when He marked out the foundations of the earth,

30 then I was beside Him, like a master workman,

and I was daily His delight,

rejoicing before Him always,

31 rejoicing in His inhabited world

and delighting in the children of man.

32 "And now, O sons, listen to me:

blessed are those who keep My ways.

33 Hear instruction and be wise,

and do not neglect it.

34 Blessed is the one who listens to Me,

watching daily at my gates,

waiting beside my doors.

35 For whoever finds Me finds life

and obtains favor from the LORD,

36 but he who fails to find Me injures himself;

all who hate Me love death."

Mark and Remark

Mark your favorite proverb above and remark why you chose it.

Life, Liberty, and the Pursuit of Happiness

Pair and Share

1. Describe the perfect vacation.

What is happiness? Hanging out? Chilling out? Many moderns regard rest as a weekend of binging on Netflix and Cheetos. But the ancients recognized rest as the liberty to pursue wisdom, specifically the liberal arts (philosophy, literature, math, and science)—arts that can be pursued only when one is free from manual labor. The liberal arts, meaning "liberty," are the kind of pursuits free people might pursue in their free time. In the Third Commandment, God gives us rest so He can go to work refreshing us and teaching us wisdom, specifically the wisdom of His Word.

4:7 The beginning of wisdom is this: Get wisdom,

and whatever you get, get insight.

8:10 Take my instruction instead of silver,

and knowledge rather than choice gold,

11 for wisdom is better than jewels,

and all that you may desire cannot compare with her.

9:1 Wisdom has built her house;

she has hewn her seven pillars.

2 She has slaughtered her beasts; she has mixed her wine;

she has also set her table.

3 She has sent out her young women to call

from the highest places in the town,

4 "Whoever is simple, let him turn in here!"

To him who lacks sense she says,

5 "Come, eat of my bread

and drink of the wine I have mixed.

6 Leave your simple ways, and live,

and walk in the way of insight."

16:16 How much better to get wisdom than gold!

To get understanding is to be chosen rather than silver.

18:15 An intelligent heart acquires knowledge,

and the ear of the wise seeks knowledge.

23:12 Apply your heart to instruction

and your ear to words of knowledge.

23:23 Buy truth, and do not sell it;

buy wisdom, instruction, and understanding.

25:2 It is the glory of God to conceal things,

> but the glory of kings is to search things out.[3]

Mark and Remark

Mark your favorite proverb above and remark why you chose it.

The Truth Shall Set You Free

Listening to lies breaks the Third Commandment. Jesus describes the devil: "He was a murderer from the beginning, and does not stand in the truth, because there is no truth in him. When he lies, he speaks out of his own character, for he is a liar and the father of lies" (John 8:44). Treasuring the truth keeps the Third Commandment. Jesus heralds Himself, "If you abide in My word, you are truly My disciples, and you will know the truth, and the truth will set you free" (John 8:31–32). Get wisdom; get insight; get Jesus.

4:5 Get wisdom; get insight;

> do not forget, and do not turn away from the words of my mouth.

6 Do not forsake her, and she will keep you;

> love her, and she will guard you.[4]

4:13 Keep hold of instruction; do not let go;

> guard her, for she is your life.

13:20 Whoever walks with the wise becomes wise,

> but the companion of fools will suffer harm.

15:14 The heart of him who has understanding seeks knowledge,

> but the mouths of fools feed on folly.

15:30 The light of the eyes rejoices the heart,

> and good news refreshes the bones.

---

3   Humans are not God, but our attributes mirror God's image. God is omniscient (Psalm 147:4–5), and God has made man intelligent, mirroring His omniscience. God in His glory knows everything, and human beings mirror His glory as they search things out.

4   *Chokmah*, Hebrew for "wisdom," is grammatically feminine. Solomon uses this grammar for wordplay, not to delineate the gender of the Second Person of the Trinity.

16:22 Good sense is a fountain of life to him who has it,

but the instruction of fools is folly.

17:24 The discerning sets his face toward wisdom,

but the eyes of a fool are on the ends of the earth.

19:8 Whoever gets sense loves his own soul;

he who keeps understanding will discover good.

20:15 There is gold and abundance of costly stones,

but the lips of knowledge are a precious jewel.

21:16 One who wanders from the way of good sense

will rest in the assembly of the dead.

25:25 Like cold water to a thirsty soul,

so is good news from a far country.

28:26 Whoever trusts in his own mind is a fool,

but he who walks in wisdom will be delivered.

Mark and Remark

Mark your favorite proverb above and remark why you chose it.

Mind Your P's and Q's

A British teacher might have said, "Mind your p's and q's" to her young students learning how to write so they wouldn't confuse the letters *p* and *q*. A British father might have said, "Mind your p's and q's" to an older son learning how to drink responsibly so he wouldn't confuse his *pints* and *quarts*. The Third Commandment commands, "Mind your p's and q's": "Live what you learn." If Tommy learns wisdom but doesn't live out that wisdom, "he is like a man who looks intently at his natural face in a mirror. For he looks at himself and goes away and at once forgets what he was like" (James 1:23–24). Minding your p's and q's means to "be doers of the word, and not hearers only" (James 1:22).

10:8 The wise of heart will receive commandments,

   but a babbling fool will come to ruin.

10:23 Doing wrong is like a joke to a fool,

   but wisdom is pleasure to a man of understanding.

13:13 Whoever despises the word brings destruction on himself,

   but he who reveres the commandment will be rewarded.

19:16 Whoever keeps the commandment keeps his life;

   he who despises his ways will die.

21:16 One who wanders from the way of good sense

   will rest in the assembly of the dead.

28:4 Those who forsake the law praise the wicked,

   but those who keep the law strive against them.

29:18 Where there is no prophetic vision the people cast off restraint,

   but blessed is he who keeps the law.[5]

Mark and Remark

Mark your favorite proverb above and remark why you chose it.

Practice What You Preach

Pair and Share

2. When was the last time you practiced what you preached? What happened?

---

5   When the cat's away, the mice will play. When God's Word is missing, Satan comes hissing.

The Third Commandment commands us to put first things first. We want to be people of integrity. Integrity is the integration of wisdom and work. Integrity is the integration of our head, heart, and hands. When the nitty hits the gritty and your hands follow through with what your head knows and your heart believes, you have integrity. When the going gets tough, the tough get going. But if I think I'm tough and have integrity, Jesus pokes and provokes, "The spirit indeed is willing but the flesh is weak" (Matthew 26:41). Keeping the Third Commandment means humbling ourselves to God's work on us through His Word and Sacraments to integrate our head, heart, and hands (John 14:26).

3:3 Let not steadfast love and faithfulness forsake you;
>
> bind them around your neck;
>
> write them on the tablet of your heart.
>
> 4 So you will find favor and good success
>
> in the sight of God and man.

10:9 Whoever walks in integrity walks securely,
>
> but he who makes his ways crooked will be found out.

11:3 The integrity of the upright guides them,
>
> but the crookedness of the treacherous destroys them.

19:1 Better is a poor person who walks in his integrity
>
> than one who is crooked in speech and is a fool.

20:6 Many a man proclaims his own steadfast love,
>
> but a faithful man who can find?
>
> 7 The righteous who walks in his integrity—
>
> blessed are his children after him!

21:22 A wise man scales the city of the mighty
>
> and brings down the stronghold in which they trust.

24:3 By wisdom a house is built,
>
> and by understanding it is established;
>
> 4 by knowledge the rooms are filled
>
> with all precious and pleasant riches.

24:10 If you faint in the day of adversity,

your strength is small.

28:18 Whoever walks in integrity will be delivered,

but he who is crooked in his ways will suddenly fall.

Mark and Remark

Mark your favorite proverb above and remark why you chose it.

Six Days You Shall Labor

The Third Commandment pairs labor with leisure, vocation with vacation, and responsibility with recreation:

> Remember the Sabbath day, to keep it holy. Six days you shall labor, and do all your work, but the seventh day is a Sabbath to the LORD your God. On it you shall not do any work, you, or your son, or your daughter, your male servant, or your female servant, or your livestock, or the sojourner who is within your gates. For in six days the LORD made heaven and earth, the sea, and all that is in them, and rested on the seventh day. Therefore the LORD blessed the Sabbath day and made it holy. (Exodus 20:8–11)

God made man in His image to mirror His plan for labor and leisure, vocation and vacation. In the Third Commandment, God commands, "Get ready to work hard and play hard, like Me." We have focused on playing hard, so now let's focus on working hard.

Idle Hands Are the Devil's Tools

Yes, all work and no play make Jack a dull boy. But all play and no work make Jack a null boy, slothful and sluggish. Because humans are made in the image of God, God commands us to mirror Him. God is a slugger, not a sluggard. But sin bogs us down and makes us sluggards. So God gives us the Third Commandment to drive us to His Word and Sacraments, where He restores His image in us and empowers us to work with joy.

6:6 Go to the ant, O sluggard;

consider her ways, and be wise.

7 Without having any chief,

officer, or ruler,

8 she prepares her bread in summer

and gathers her food in harvest.

10:26 Like vinegar to the teeth and smoke to the eyes,

so is the sluggard to those who send him.

13:4 The soul of the sluggard craves and gets nothing,

while the soul of the diligent is richly supplied.

15:19 The way of a sluggard is like a hedge of thorns,

but the path of the upright is a level highway.

19:24 The sluggard buries his hand in the dish

and will not even bring it back to his mouth.

20:4 The sluggard does not plow in the autumn;

he will seek at harvest and have nothing.

21:25 The desire of the sluggard kills him,

for his hands refuse to labor.

26 All day long he craves and craves,

but the righteous gives and does not hold back.

22:13 The sluggard says, "There is a lion outside!

I shall be killed in the streets!"

26:13 The sluggard says, "There is a lion in the road!

There is a lion in the streets!"

26:15 The sluggard buries his hand in the dish;

it wears him out to bring it back to his mouth.

16 The sluggard is wiser in his own eyes

than seven men who can answer sensibly.

Mark and Remark

Mark your favorite proverb above and remark why you chose it.

Early to Bed and Early to Rise

Pair and Share

3. Are you a night owl or a morning dove? What healthy habits help you make the most of your day?

6:9 How long will you lie there, O sluggard?

When will you arise from your sleep?

10 A little sleep, a little slumber,

a little folding of the hands to rest,

11 and poverty will come upon you like a robber,

and want like an armed man.

19:15 Slothfulness casts into a deep sleep,

and an idle person will suffer hunger.

20:13 Love not sleep, lest you come to poverty;

open your eyes, and you will have plenty of bread.

24:30 I passed by the field of a sluggard,

by the vineyard of a man lacking sense,

31 and behold, it was all overgrown with thorns;

the ground was covered with nettles,

and its stone wall was broken down.

32 Then I saw and considered it;

I looked and received instruction.

33 A little sleep, a little slumber,

    a little folding of the hands to rest,

34 and poverty will come upon you like a robber,

    and want like an armed man.

26:14 As a door turns on its hinges,

    so does a sluggard on his bed.

Mark and Remark

Mark your favorite proverb above and remark why you chose it.

Keep Your Nose to the Grindstone

Made in God's image, humans were made to have dominion over His dominion with Him (Genesis 1:26). Because we are made in His image, God commands humans in the Third Commandment to mirror His work ethic: "Six days you shall labor, and do all your work. . . . For in six days the LORD made heaven and earth" (Exodus 20:9, 11). Made in God's image and re-created in Christ's image, humans were made to work (John 4:34).

10:5 He who gathers in summer is a prudent son,

    but he who sleeps in harvest is a son who brings shame.

18:9 Whoever is slack in his work

    is a brother to him who destroys.

21:26 All day long he [the sluggard] craves and craves,

    but the righteous gives and does not hold back.

27:23 Know well the condition of your flocks,

    and give attention to your herds,

24 for riches do not last forever;

    and does a crown endure to all generations?

Mark and Remark

Mark your favorite proverb above and remark why you chose it.

A Cat in Gloves Catches No Mice

For us and for our salvation, Christ came down from heaven, laid His head in a manger, and got His hands dirty for us. For us and for our sanctification, the Holy Spirit comes down from heaven, makes His home in our heart, and gets us ready to get our hands dirty.

14:4 Where there are no oxen, the manger is clean,

> but abundant crops come by the strength of the ox.

Hard Work Never Hurt Anybody

Hard work will hurt everybody if we try to work for our salvation. "For by grace you have been saved through faith. And this is not your own doing; it is the gift of God, not a result of works, so that no one may boast" (Ephesians 2:8–9). You boast, you're toast. But after the Holy Spirit calls, gathers, and enlightens us with God the Father's grace in His Son, Jesus Christ, then the Holy Spirit sanctifies us for hard work: "For we are His workmanship, created in Christ Jesus for good works, which God prepared beforehand, that we should walk in them" (Ephesians 2:10).[6]

12:24 The hand of the diligent will rule,

> while the slothful will be put to forced labor.

12:27 Whoever is slothful will not roast his game,

> but the diligent man will get precious wealth.

14:23 In all toil there is profit,

> but mere talk tends only to poverty.

22:29 Do you see a man skillful in his work?

---

6   See Epitome IV 5–15.

He will stand before kings;

he will not stand before obscure men.

27:18 Whoever tends a fig tree will eat its fruit,

and he who guards his master will be honored.

28:19 Whoever works his land will have plenty of bread,

but he who follows worthless pursuits will have plenty of poverty.

Mark and Remark

Mark your favorite proverb above and remark why you chose it.

Personalize and Memorize

"Hold it sacred and gladly hear and learn it." With the Holy Spirit's help (John 14:26; Romans 8:11), keeping the Third Commandment means humbling ourselves to let God go to work forgiving us, restoring us, and teaching us His wisdom. Remembering that salvation is the gift of God and not a result of works, analyze all the Third Commandment proverbs you previously marked and choose your favorite. Which proverb will help you keep the Third Commandment with fear, love, and trust because you are baptized—because you are created in Christ—because God the Father forgives, loves, and treasures you in His Son first? Memorize it. Imagine a moment this week when you'll utilize your proverb. It will be pleasant if you keep it within you, if it is always ready on your lips (Proverbs 22:18).

We thank You, kind Father, that You give us time to hear Your Holy Word. Grant that fearing and loving You, we may set aside our work to receive Your Son's words, which are spirit and life, and so, refreshed and renewed by the preaching of Your Gospel, we might live in the peace and quietness that come through faith alone; we ask it for the sake of Jesus Christ, our Lord. Amen.[7]

---

7   *Luther's Small Catechism with Explanation*, Third Commandment, prayer.

CHAPTER 4

THE FOURTH COMMANDMENT

Honor your father and your mother. *What does this mean?* We should fear and love God so that we do not despise or anger our parents and other authorities, but honor them, serve and obey them, love and cherish them.

Deep Memory

Dig deep and ink your First through Third Commandment proverbs.

Honor Your Father and Your Mother

Pair and Share

1. "We are His workmanship, created in Christ Jesus for good works, which God prepared beforehand, that we should walk in them" (Ephesians 2:10). When you think of a Christian good work you could do, what comes to mind first?

Commandments One through Three (the First Table) show us how to fear, love, and trust in God above all things. Commandments Four through Ten (the Second Table) show us how to honor, love, and cherish our neighbor as ourselves (Mark 12:30–31). From the Second Table, would you believe the greatest Christian good work you can do is to honor your father and mother? Luther teaches that the Fourth Commandment is the foremost commandment of the Second Table:

> This is the highest work we can do, after the grand divine worship included in the previous commandments. Giving to the poor and every other good work toward our neighbor is not equal to this. For God has assigned parenthood the highest place. Yes, He has set it up in His own place upon the earth. God's will and pleasure ought to be enough reason and incentive for us to do what we can with good will and pleasure.[1]

When you thought of your Christian good work, was honoring your father and mother the first thing that came to mind? How come we forget about our parents? The same way we forget God. Just as we forget God's providence and protection, so we forget our parents' providence and protection.[2]

> God knows very well this perverseness of the world; therefore, He admonishes and urges by commandments that everyone consider what his parents have done for him. Each child will discover that he has from them a body and life. He has been fed and reared when otherwise he would have perished a hundred times in his own filth.[3]

Think and Ink

2. Consider what your parents or another significant adult in your life has done for you. Not all of us have had loving parents. When you consider the love and care of your parents or another significant adult, what comes to mind first?

Charity Begins at Home

There are two sides to the coin of the Fourth Commandment. Yes, children are to honor, love, and cherish their parents (Ephesians 6:1–3). But parents are to honor, love, and cherish their children even more, "bring[ing] them

---

1   Large Catechism I 125–26.
2   Large Catechism I 128.
3   Large Catechism I 129.

up in the discipline and instruction of the Lord" (Ephesians 6:4). Parents not only put food on the table but also teach the First and Second Tables. "Charity begins at home" because parents are to teach their children to fear, love, and trust in God first and to honor, love, and cherish their neighbor second.

Think and Ink

3. Read Deuteronomy 6:4–7. How often should parents teach their children Law and Gospel?

> 1:8 Hear, my son, your father's instruction,
>> and forsake not your mother's teaching,
> 9 for they are a graceful garland for your head
>> and pendants for your neck.
>
> 3:1 My son, do not forget my teaching,
>> but let your heart keep my commandments,
> 2 for length of days and years of life
>> and peace they will add to you.
>
> 4:1 Hear, O sons, a father's instruction,
>> and be attentive, that you may gain insight,
> 2 for I give you good precepts;
>> do not forsake my teaching.
> 3 When I was a son with my father,
>> tender, the only one in the sight of my mother,
> 4 he taught me and said to me,
>> "Let your heart hold fast my words;
>> keep my commandments, and live."
>
> 4:20 My son, be attentive to my words;
>> incline your ear to my sayings.
> 21 Let them not escape from your sight;
>> keep them within your heart.

22 For they are life to those who find them,

    and healing to all their flesh.

5:1 My son, be attentive to my wisdom;

    incline your ear to my understanding,

2 that you may keep discretion,

    and your lips may guard knowledge.

6:20 My son, keep your father's commandment,

    and forsake not your mother's teaching.

21 Bind them on your heart always;

    tie them around your neck.

22 When you walk, they will lead you;

    when you lie down, they will watch over you;

    and when you awake, they will talk with you.

23 For the commandment is a lamp and the teaching a light,

    and the reproofs of discipline are the way of life.

7:1 My son, keep my words

    and treasure up my commandments with you;

2 keep my commandments and live;

    keep my teaching as the apple of your eye;

3 bind them on your fingers;

    write them on the tablet of your heart.

22:28 Do not move the ancient landmark

    that your fathers have set.[4]

23:22 Listen to your father who gave you life,

    and do not despise your mother when she is old.

Mark and Remark

Mark your favorite proverb above and remark why you chose it.

---

4   The arrogant could arrogate land by moving markers. "The meek . . . shall inherit the earth" (Matthew 5:5).

Spare the Rod, Spoil the Child

Pair and Share

4. How did your parents discipline you? If you are a parent, how do you discipline your children?

Think and Ink

5. Read Hebrews 12:5–11. Put it in your own words. Sum it all up with a pithy sentence.

God disciplines us with the Law and delights us with the Gospel because He loves us. Likewise, Christian parents should discipline and delight with the same Law and Gospel, curbing our sin, punishing our sin, forgiving our sin, and giving us guidance because they love us.

> 3:11 My son, do not despise the LORD's discipline
>> or be weary of His reproof,
>
> 12 for the LORD reproves him whom He loves,
>> as a father the son in whom he delights.
>
> 13:24 Whoever spares the rod hates his son,
>> but he who loves him is diligent to discipline him.
>
> 19:18 Discipline your son, for there is hope;
>> do not set your heart on putting him to death.[5]

---

5   Deuteronomy 21:18–21 permits the death penalty for stubborn and rebellious children who will not submit to discipline. When God gives the Fourth Commandment (Exodus 20:12), He immediately confirms it with the capital consequence for breaking it (Exodus 21:15, 17). The story of Eli and his wicked sons reveals that God is dead serious about fathers disciplining their sons (1 Samuel 2:12–36; 3:11–14).

20:30 Blows that wound cleanse away evil;

strokes make clean the innermost parts.

22:15 Folly is bound up in the heart of a child,

but the rod of discipline drives it far from him.

23:13 Do not withhold discipline from a child;

if you strike him with a rod, he will not die.

14 If you strike him with the rod,

you will save his soul from Sheol.

29:15 The rod and reproof give wisdom,

but a child left to himself brings shame to his mother.

29:17 Discipline your son, and he will give you rest;

he will give delight to your heart.

29:19 By mere words a servant is not disciplined,

for though he understands, he will not respond.

Mark and Remark

Mark your favorite proverb above and remark why you chose it.

There's a Black Sheep in Every Family

Did you know it's nearly impossible to despise your parents and love your life at the same time? The Fourth Commandment is the first commandment with a promise: "that it may go well with you and that you may live long in the land" (Ephesians 6:1–3; see also Exodus 20:12). Luther explains:

> Whoever keeps this commandment shall have happy days, fortune, and prosperity. On the other hand, . . . whoever is disobedient shall perish sooner and never enjoy life. For to have long life in the sense of the Scriptures is not only to become old, but to have everything that belongs to long life: health, wife, children, livelihood, peace, good

government, and so on. Without these things this life can neither be enjoyed in cheerfulness nor long endure. If, therefore, you will not obey father and mother and submit to their discipline, then obey the hangman. If you will not obey him, then submit to the skeleton man (i.e., death).[6]

11:29 Whoever troubles his own household will inherit the wind,
> and the fool will be servant to the wise of heart.

17:21 He who sires a fool gets himself sorrow,
> and the father of a fool has no joy.

17:25 A foolish son is a grief to his father
> and bitterness to her who bore him.

19:26 He who does violence to his father and chases away his mother
> is a son who brings shame and reproach.

20:20 If one curses his father or his mother,
> his lamp will be put out in utter darkness.

28:24 Whoever robs his father or his mother
> and says, "That is no transgression,"
> is a companion to a man who destroys.

30:17 The eye that mocks a father
> and scorns to obey a mother
will be picked out by the ravens of the valley
> and eaten by the vultures.

Mark and Remark

Mark your favorite proverb above and remark why you chose it.

---

6   Large Catechism I 134.

The Apple Doesn't Fall Far from the Tree

Like father, like son. Like mother, like daughter. Children often take after the nature and nurture of their parents.

10:1 A wise son makes a glad father,

but a foolish son is a sorrow to his mother.

15:20 A wise son makes a glad father,

but a foolish man despises his mother.

20:11 Even a child makes himself known by his acts,

by whether his conduct is pure and upright.

22:6 Train up a child in the way he should go;

even when he is old he will not depart from it.

23:15 My son, if your heart is wise,

my heart too will be glad.

23:24 The father of the righteous will greatly rejoice;

he who fathers a wise son will be glad in him.

25 Let your father and mother be glad;

let her who bore you rejoice.

28:7 The one who keeps the law is a son with understanding,

but a companion of gluttons shames his father.

Mark and Remark

Mark your favorite proverb above and remark why you chose it.

Don't Bite the Hand That Feeds You

Pair and Share

6. "Never trust anyone over thirty." How does our culture idolize youth and minimize maturity?

"Yes, sir." "No, sir." "Yes, ma'am." "No, ma'am." If you grow up in the Deep South, you know that honoring your parents, elders, and authorities with these honorifics is the norm. When I received my first call to Nebraska and honored my Midwestern parishioners with the same "Yes, sir" and "Yes, ma'am," they were startled, but they never told me to stop. None of us would be here today without the providence and protection of parents, elders, and authorities who came before us. Don't bite the hand that feeds you. Honor them, serve and obey them, love and cherish them.

16:31 Gray hair is a crown of glory;
>   it is gained in a righteous life.

17:6 Grandchildren are the crown of the aged,
>   and the glory of children is their fathers.

20:29 The glory of young men is their strength,
>   but the splendor of old men is their gray hair.

Mark and Remark

Mark your favorite proverb above and remark why you chose it.

Two Heads Are Better Than One

When we honor our parents and other authorities, we obey their good guidance, and by doing so, we become teachable and amenable—wise people who ask for and receive advice. The weird word *synod* in The Lutheran Church—Missouri Synod comes from the Greek prefix *syn*, meaning "together," and the Greek word *hodos*, meaning "way, road, or path." Christ is the *hodos*, "the way, and the truth, and the life" (John 14:6). Called and gathered by the Holy Spirit, Missouri Synod Lutherans "walk the way of Christ together." Some say, "If you want something done right, do it yourself." But the Body of Christ always works better by walking together (1 Corinthians 12:12, 21).

9:9 Give instruction to a wise man, and he will be still wiser;

teach a righteous man, and he will increase in learning.

11:14 Where there is no guidance, a people falls,

but in an abundance of counselors there is safety.

12:15 The way of a fool is right in his own eyes,

but a wise man listens to advice.

13:10 By insolence comes nothing but strife,

but with those who take advice is wisdom.

13:14 The teaching of the wise is a fountain of life,

that one may turn away from the snares of death.

13:20 Whoever walks with the wise becomes wise,

but the companion of fools will suffer harm.

15:22 Without counsel plans fail,

but with many advisers they succeed.

17:17 A friend loves at all times,

and a brother is born for adversity.

18:1 Whoever isolates himself seeks his own desire;

he breaks out against all sound judgment.

18:24 A man of many companions may come to ruin,

but there is a friend who sticks closer than a brother.

19:20 Listen to advice and accept instruction,

    that you may gain wisdom in the future.

19:27 Cease to hear instruction, my son,

    and you will stray from the words of knowledge.

20:18 Plans are established by counsel;

    by wise guidance wage war.

22:17 Incline your ear, and hear the words of the wise,

    and apply your heart to my knowledge,

18 for it will be pleasant if you keep them within you,

    if all of them are ready on your lips.

27:9 Oil and perfume make the heart glad,

    and the sweetness of a friend comes from his earnest counsel.

27:17 Iron sharpens iron,

    and one man sharpens another.

Mark and Remark

Mark your favorite proverb above and remark why you chose it.

Live and Learn

Think and Ink

7. Some friends tell you what you want to hear, but your best friends tell you what you need to hear. What was the last constructive critique you received? How did you receive it?

Keeping the Fourth Commandment with the Holy Spirit's help means learning how to live and learn, learning from our mistakes. Iron sharpens iron in the Book of Acts when Priscilla and Aquilla sharpen Apollos. Read Acts 18:24–28. What is so sharp about Apollos is not how sharp he is but how able he is to be sharpened. Help us, Holy Spirit, to live and learn.

9:8 Do not reprove a scoffer, or he will hate you;

reprove a wise man, and he will love you.

10:17 Whoever heeds instruction is on the path to life,

but he who rejects reproof leads others astray.

12:1 Whoever loves discipline loves knowledge,

but he who hates reproof is stupid.

13:1 A wise son hears his father's instruction,

but a scoffer does not listen to rebuke.

13:18 Poverty and disgrace come to him who ignores instruction,

but whoever heeds reproof is honored.

15:5 A fool despises his father's instruction,

but whoever heeds reproof is prudent.

15:10 There is severe discipline for him who forsakes the way;

whoever hates reproof will die.

15:12 A scoffer does not like to be reproved;

he will not go to the wise.

15:31 The ear that listens to life-giving reproof

will dwell among the wise.

32 Whoever ignores instruction despises himself,

but he who listens to reproof gains intelligence.

17:10 A rebuke goes deeper into a man of understanding

than a hundred blows into a fool.

25:12 Like a gold ring or an ornament of gold

is a wise reprover to a listening ear.

27:5 Better is open rebuke

than hidden love.

28:23 Whoever rebukes a man will afterward find more favor

than he who flatters with his tongue.

29:1 He who is often reproved, yet stiffens his neck,

will suddenly be broken beyond healing.

Mark and Remark

Mark your favorite proverb above and remark why you chose it.

Render to Caesar the Things That Are Caesar's

"We should fear and love God so that we do not despise or anger our parents *and other authorities*" (emphasis added). To provide His providence and protection, God has instituted seven heads with His authority. First and foremost, Christ is the head of His Body, the Church (Ephesians 5:23). Husbands are the heads of their wives (Ephesians 5:22–33). Parents are the heads of their children (Ephesians 6:1–4). Teachers are the heads of their students (John 13:13–14). Masters (bosses) are the heads of their servants (workers) (Ephesians 6:5–9). Pastors are the heads of their flocks (Hebrews 13:17). And the government is the head of its citizens (Romans 13:1–7). All of us are to honor, love, and cherish all seven of these God-given authorities, and we owe them our obedience, except if they were to command us to sin (Acts 5:29).[7] The other side of the coin of the Fourth Commandment is that all of these authorities are obliged to honor, love, and cherish their subjects even more. The Church does not honor, love, and cherish Christ more than Christ honors, loves, and cherishes the Church. So husbands, parents, teachers, masters, pastors, and governments should love their wives, children, students, servants, flock, and citizens as Christ loves the Church (Ephesians 5:25).

---

7   Augsburg Confession XVI 6–7.

Think and Ink

8. Read Romans 13:1–7. Why should Christians submit to the authorities, or render to Caesar the things that are Caesar's?

14:28 In a multitude of people is the glory of a king,
    but without people a prince is ruined.

14:35 A servant who deals wisely has the king's favor,
    but his wrath falls on one who acts shamefully.

16:12 It is an abomination to kings to do evil,
    for the throne is established by righteousness.

16:14 A king's wrath is a messenger of death,
    and a wise man will appease it.

19:12 A king's wrath is like the growling of a lion,
    but his favor is like dew on the grass.

20:2 The terror of a king is like the growling of a lion;
    whoever provokes him to anger forfeits his life.

20:8 A king who sits on the throne of judgment
    winnows all evil with his eyes.

20:26 A wise king winnows the wicked
    and drives the wheel over them.

20:28 Steadfast love and faithfulness preserve the king,
    and by steadfast love his throne is upheld.

25:6 Do not put yourself forward in the king's presence
    or stand in the place of the great,
7 for it is better to be told, "Come up here,"
    than to be put lower in the presence of a noble.

28:15 Like a roaring lion or a charging bear

is a wicked ruler over a poor people.

16 A ruler who lacks understanding is a cruel oppressor,

but he who hates unjust gain will prolong his days.

29:4 By justice a king builds up the land,

but he who exacts gifts tears it down.

29:12 If a ruler listens to falsehood,

all his officials will be wicked.

29:14 If a king faithfully judges the poor,

his throne will be established forever.

Mark and Remark

Mark your favorite proverb above and remark why you chose it.

Personalize and Memorize

"Honor them, serve and obey them, love and cherish them." With the Holy Spirit's help (John 14:26; Romans 8:11), keeping the Fourth Commandment means honoring our parents and other authorities through whom God provides His providence and protection. Analyze all the Fourth Commandment proverbs you previously marked and choose your favorite. Which proverb will help you keep the Fourth Commandment with fear, love, and trust because you are baptized—because you are created in Christ—because God the Father forgives, loves, and treasures you in His Son first? Memorize it. Imagine a moment this week when you'll utilize your proverb. It will be pleasant if you keep it within you, if it is always ready on your lips (Proverbs 22:18).

Heavenly Father, from whom all fatherhood on earth is given: give unto us gratitude for the gifts of parents and others in authority and the humility to serve, obey, love, and cherish them as they fulfill the duties and responsibilities You have assigned to them in this life; through Your Son, Jesus Christ, our Lord. Amen.[8]

---

8   *Luther's Small Catechism with Explanation*, Fourth Commandment, prayer.

CHAPTER 5

THE FIFTH COMMANDMENT

You shall not murder. *What does this mean?* We should fear and love God so that we do not hurt or harm our neighbor in his body, but help and support him in every physical need.

Deep Memory

Dig deep and ink your First through Fourth Commandment proverbs.

Hurt and Harm or Help and Support

Honoring, loving, and cherishing our parents and other authorities keeps the Fourth Commandment. Honoring, loving, and cherishing our neighbor in his or her body keeps the Fifth Commandment. It seems like common sense, but how do I know when I am not hurting or harming but helping and supporting my neighbor?

Pair and Share

1. What is the definition of a table? Google it.

When you look up the definition of anything, whether a creation of God, like a honeybee, or an invention of man, like a table, the definition always defines a thing's form and function. The form tells us what a thing is, and the function tells us its purpose. The form of a honeybee is that it is a flying insect, and its function is to make honey. The form of a table is that it is a piece of furniture with a flat top and one or more legs, and its function is to provide a flat surface on which objects may be placed, that can be used for eating, writing, or working. A good table is able to fulfill this function; a bad table is unable to fulfill this function. If one of a table's legs is broken and the surface isn't flat enough for eating, writing, or working, then it is a bad table. If a form cannot fulfill its function, it is bad.

If I came into a classroom one morning and found all the tables turned over, would I say a harmful or helpful person did this? A harmful person did this. Why is that person harmful? Because that person turned over the tables so that they could not fulfill their function, which hurts and harms me. It is not meet, right, or salutary for me to eat, write, or work on a table that has been turned over.

With all things, whether creations of God or inventions of man, if I hurt or hinder them from fulfilling their functions, then I am hurtful and harmful. Turning over tables in a classroom breaks the Fifth Commandment. But if you help and support things in fulfilling their functions, then you are helpful and supportive. Turning the tables back over keeps the Fifth Commandment.

What about helping and supporting your neighbor, a human being? It all depends on the function of a human being. What is our function? God writes this function on our hearts (Romans 2:14–15) and sets it in stone on two tables (Exodus 20:1–17). Your function is, first, to fear, love, and trust in God above all things and, second, to honor, love, and cherish your neighbor as yourself (Mark 12:30–31). If I help and support you in fulfilling these two functions, then I am helpful and supportive. If I hurt or hinder you from fulfilling these, I am hurtful and harmful.

Think and Ink

2. Sum it all up with a pithy sentence. How do you know you are not hurting or harming but helping and supporting your neighbor?

A Good Man Is Hard to Find

In our fallen, sinful world, the peer pressure to break the Fifth Commandment and hurt and harm is high. Peter pushes back:

> Live for the rest of the time in the flesh no longer for human passions but for the will of God. For the time that is past suffices for doing what the Gentiles want to do, living in sensuality, passions, drunkenness, orgies, drinking parties, and lawless idolatry. With respect to this they are surprised when you do not join them in the same flood of debauchery, and they malign you; but they will give account to Him who is ready to judge the living and the dead. (1 Peter 4:2–5)

4:14 Do not enter the path of the wicked,
　　and do not walk in the way of the evil.
15 Avoid it; do not go on it;
　　turn away from it and pass on.
16 For they cannot sleep unless they have done wrong;
　　they are robbed of sleep unless they have made someone stumble.
17 For they eat the bread of wickedness
　　and drink the wine of violence.
18 But the path of the righteous is like the light of dawn,
　　which shines brighter and brighter until full day.
19 The way of the wicked is like deep darkness;
　　they do not know over what they stumble.

12:26 One who is righteous is a guide to his neighbor,
　　but the way of the wicked leads them astray.

16:29 A man of violence entices his neighbor
　　and leads him in a way that is not good.

21:10 The soul of the wicked desires evil;
　　his neighbor finds no mercy in his eyes.

28:28 When the wicked rise, people hide themselves,
　　but when they perish, the righteous increase.

29:2 When the righteous increase, the people rejoice,
　　but when the wicked rule, the people groan.

29:10 Bloodthirsty men hate one who is blameless

and seek the life of the upright.

Mark and Remark

Mark your favorite proverb above and remark why you chose it.

Crime Doesn't Pay

When I hurt or harm my neighbors instead of helping and supporting them, I am wicked. The reason I break the Fifth Commandment is because I sinfully and selfishly deceive myself, believing my wickedness will help and support me. Paul pushes back, "Do not be deceived: God is not mocked, for whatever one sows, that will he also reap" (Galatians 6:7). Sooner or later, the chickens will come home to roost.

3:33 The LORD's curse is on the house of the wicked,

but He blesses the dwelling of the righteous.

5:22 The iniquities of the wicked ensnare him,

and he is held fast in the cords of his sin.

10:24 What the wicked dreads will come upon him,

but the desire of the righteous will be granted.

10:28 The hope of the righteous brings joy,

but the expectation of the wicked will perish.

11:19 Whoever is steadfast in righteousness will live,

but he who pursues evil will die.

11:20 Those of crooked heart are an abomination to the LORD,

but those of blameless ways are His delight.

11:23 The desire of the righteous ends only in good,

the expectation of the wicked in wrath.

11:31 If the righteous is repaid on earth,

how much more the wicked and the sinner!

12:3 No one is established by wickedness,

but the root of the righteous will never be moved.

12:7 The wicked are overthrown and are no more,

but the house of the righteous will stand.

13:9 The light of the righteous rejoices,

but the lamp of the wicked will be put out.

14:11 The house of the wicked will be destroyed,

but the tent of the upright will flourish.

15:9 The way of the wicked is an abomination to the LORD,

but He loves him who pursues righteousness.

16:4 The LORD has made everything for its purpose,

even the wicked for the day of trouble.[1]

17:13 If anyone returns evil for good,

evil will not depart from his house.

18:3 When wickedness comes, contempt comes also,

and with dishonor comes disgrace.

21:7 The violence of the wicked will sweep them away,

because they refuse to do what is just.

21:12 The Righteous One observes the house of the wicked;

He throws the wicked down to ruin.

21:27 The sacrifice of the wicked is an abomination;

how much more when he brings it with evil intent.

22:8 Whoever sows injustice will reap calamity,

and the rod of his fury will fail.

---

1   God is not the author or cause of wickedness; the devil, the world, and our sinful nature are (James 1:13–14). Second Peter 3:9 consoles that the Lord "is patient toward you, not wishing that any should perish, but that all should reach repentance." But 2 Peter 3:10 confirms that the Lord will one day come like a thief in the night to judge the wicked and redeem the faithful.

26:27 Whoever digs a pit will fall into it,

and a stone will come back on him who starts it rolling.

28:17 If one is burdened with the blood of another,

he will be a fugitive until death;

let no one help him.

29:6 An evil man is ensnared in his transgression,

but a righteous man sings and rejoices.

29:16 When the wicked increase, transgression increases,

but the righteous will look upon their downfall.

Mark and Remark

Mark your favorite proverb above and remark why you chose it.

Don't Let the Fox Guard the Henhouse

Don't assign a weighty task to a wicked person with a history of hurting and harming. Yes, Jesus loves Pharisees and Sadducees, but He still warns, "Beware of the leaven of the Pharisees and Sadducees" (Matthew 16:6). Past behavior is the best predictor of future behavior.

13:17 A wicked messenger falls into trouble,

but a faithful envoy brings healing.

25:19 Trusting in a treacherous man in time of trouble

is like a bad tooth or a foot that slips.

26:11 Like a dog that returns to his vomit

is a fool who repeats his folly.

28:1 The wicked flee when no one pursues,

but the righteous are bold as a lion.

Mark and Remark

Mark your favorite proverb above and remark why you chose it.

Keep Your Nose Clean

"I appeal to you therefore, brothers, by the mercies of God, to present your bodies as a living sacrifice, holy and acceptable to God, which is your spiritual worship. Do not be conformed to this world, but be transformed by the renewal of your mind, that by testing you may discern what is the will of God, what is good and acceptable and perfect" (Romans 12:1–2). Keep your nose clean.

3:29 Do not plan evil against your neighbor,
>who dwells trustingly beside you.

30 Do not contend with a man for no reason,
>when he has done you no harm.

31 Do not envy a man of violence
>and do not choose any of his ways,

32 for the devious person is an abomination to the LORD,
>but the upright are in His confidence.

12:10 Whoever is righteous has regard for the life of his beast,
>but the mercy of the wicked is cruel.[2]

21:21 Whoever pursues righteousness and kindness
>will find life, righteousness, and honor.

24:1 Be not envious of evil men,
>nor desire to be with them,

2 for their hearts devise violence,
>and their lips talk of trouble.

24:15 Lie not in wait as a wicked man against the dwelling of the righteous;
>do no violence to his home;

---

2   Made in God's image, humans mirror God's care for His creation (Matthew 6:25–33).

¹⁶ for the righteous falls seven times and rises again,

but the wicked stumble in times of calamity.

Mark and Remark

Mark your favorite proverb above and remark why you chose it.

Justice Is Blind

"Why does your teacher eat with tax collectors and sinners?" the Pharisees asked Jesus' disciples (Matthew 9:11). Jesus stands up to the wicked who puff themselves up by putting others down. "Those who are well have no need of a physician, but those who are sick. . . . I came not to call the righteous, but sinners" (Matthew 9:12–13). In the Spirit of Christ, keeping the Fifth Commandment also means breaking and hindering every evil plan and purpose of the devil, the world, and our sinful nature that would hurt and harm our neighbor.

18:5 It is not good to be partial to the wicked

or to deprive the righteous of justice.

21:3 To do righteousness and justice

is more acceptable to the LORD than sacrifice.

24:24 Whoever says to the wicked, "You are in the right,"

will be cursed by peoples, abhorred by nations,

25 but those who rebuke the wicked will have delight,

and a good blessing will come upon them.

25:26 Like a muddied spring or a polluted fountain

is a righteous man who gives way before the wicked.

28:4 Those who forsake the law praise the wicked,

but those who keep the law strive against them.

5 Evil men do not understand justice,

but those who seek the LORD understand it completely.

29:27 An unjust man is an abomination to the righteous,

but one whose way is straight is an abomination to the wicked.

31:8 Open your mouth for the mute,

for the rights of all who are destitute.

9 Open your mouth, judge righteously,

defend the rights of the poor and needy.

Mark and Remark

Mark your favorite proverb above and remark why you chose it.

Don't Blow Your Top

Think and Ink

3. Read Matthew 5:21–22. How does Jesus teach that it is possible to break the Fifth Commandment in thought and word, not only in deed?

People never hurt or harm with their hands unless they have anger and hatred in their heart. "Put on then, as God's chosen ones, holy and beloved, compassionate hearts, kindness, humility, meekness, and patience, bearing with one another and, if one has a complaint against another, forgiving each other; as the Lord has forgiven you, so you also must forgive" (Colossians 3:12–13). Keeping the Fifth Commandment with our hands means keeping it with our heart first. "Let the peace of Christ rule in your hearts" (Colossians 3:15).

10:12 Hatred stirs up strife,

but love covers all offenses.

11:17 A man who is kind benefits himself,

but a cruel man hurts himself.

14:17 A man of quick temper acts foolishly,

and a man of evil devices is hated.

19:19 A man of great wrath will pay the penalty,

for if you deliver him, you will only have to do it again.

22:24 Make no friendship with a man given to anger,

nor go with a wrathful man,

25 lest you learn his ways

and entangle yourself in a snare.

25:28 A man without self-control

is like a city broken into and left without walls.

29:22 A man of wrath stirs up strife,

and one given to anger causes much transgression.

Mark and Remark

Mark your favorite proverb above and remark why you chose it.

Still Waters Run Deep

God never says, "Do as I say, not as I do." God made humans in His image to mirror Him, and the Fifth Commandment mirrors His deep mercy and grace. "The LORD is merciful and gracious, slow to anger and abounding in steadfast love" (Psalm 103:8).

14:29 Whoever is slow to anger has great understanding,

but he who has a hasty temper exalts folly.

15:17 Better is a dinner of herbs where love is

than a fattened ox and hatred with it.

¹⁸ A hot-tempered man stirs up strife,

but he who is slow to anger quiets contention.

^{16:32} Whoever is slow to anger is better than the mighty,

and he who rules his spirit than he who takes a city.

^{17:1} Better is a dry morsel with quiet

than a house full of feasting with strife.

^{17:27} Whoever restrains his words has knowledge,

and he who has a cool spirit is a man of understanding.

^{19:11} Good sense makes one slow to anger,

and it is his glory to overlook an offense.

^{29:11} A fool gives full vent to his spirit,

but a wise man quietly holds it back.

Mark and Remark

Mark your favorite proverb above and remark why you chose it.

Two Wrongs Don't Make a Right

Pair and Share

4. Read Romans 12:17–21. What does it mean to heap hot coals on your enemy's head?

Jesus says, "You have heard that it was said, 'You shall love your neighbor and hate your enemy.' But I say to you, Love your enemies and pray for those who persecute you, so that you may be sons of your Father who is in heaven"

(Matthew 5:43–45). Jesus takes the Fifth Commandment to the limit when He cries from the cross, "Father, forgive them, for they know not what they do" (Luke 23:34).

> **20:22** Do not say, "I will repay evil";
>
> wait for the LORD, and He will deliver you.

> **24:17** Do not rejoice when your enemy falls,
>
> and let not your heart be glad when he stumbles,
>
> **18** lest the LORD see it and be displeased,
>
> and turn away His anger from him.

> **24:29** Do not say, "I will do to him as he has done to me;
>
> I will pay the man back for what he has done."

> **25:21** If your enemy is hungry, give him bread to eat,
>
> and if he is thirsty, give him water to drink,
>
> **22** for you will heap burning coals on his head,
>
> and the LORD will reward you.

Mark and Remark

Mark your favorite proverb above and remark why you chose it.

Personalize and Memorize

"Help and support him in every physical need." With the Holy Spirit's help (John 14:26; Romans 8:11), keeping the Fifth Commandment means fearing, loving, and trusting in God so that we honor, love, and cherish our neighbors in their body and life. Analyze all the Fifth Commandment proverbs you previously marked and choose your favorite. Which proverb will help you keep the Fifth Commandment with fear, love, and trust because you are baptized—because you are created in Christ—because God the Father forgives, loves, and treasures you in His Son first? Memorize it. Imagine a moment this week when you'll utilize your proverb. It will be pleasant if you keep it within you, if it is always ready on your lips (Proverbs 22:18).

Lord God, by Your Law You guard and defend every human life from violence and destruction. Give us wisdom never to hurt or harm our neighbors in their bodily life and give us hearts of mercy to help and support them in every physical need; through Jesus Christ, our Lord. Amen.[3]

---

3 *Luther's Small Catechism with Explanation*, Fifth Commandment, prayer.

CHAPTER 6

THE SIXTH COMMANDMENT

You shall not commit adultery. *What does this mean?* We should fear and love God so that we lead a sexually pure and decent life in what we say and do, and husband and wife love and honor each other.

Deep Memory

Dig deep and ink your First through Fifth Commandment proverbs.

Leave, Cleave, and Weave

Think and Ink

1. Who is worthy of your hand in marriage? What are the top three qualities a prospective spouse should have before you would marry that person? If you're married, what did you look for in your spouse?

God's prescription and description of marriage occurs three times in the Bible: Genesis 2:18–25 [2:24]; Matthew 19:3–9 [19:5]; and Ephesians 5:25–33 [5:31]): "Therefore a man shall leave his father and his mother and hold fast to his wife, and they shall become one flesh." Leave, cleave, and weave. This is God's biblical prescription and description of marriage.

1. Leave—to forsake all other human beings for supreme spiritual, mental, emotional, and physical support, to pledge one's faithfulness, and to remain united to one spouse alone.

2. Cleave—to have and to hold one spouse for better, for worse, for richer, for poorer, in sickness and in health as Christ loves the Church, not only when life is healthy and wealthy.

3. Weave—to become one flesh spiritually, mentally, emotionally, and physically with one spouse.

Pair and Share

2. Leave, cleave, and weave. What happens when two people weave physically before they leave and cleave spiritually, mentally, and emotionally?

When Christ touches people, He always touches to heal (Mark 1:40–42), feed (Mark 6:38–44), and bless (Mark 10:13–16), not to hurt, take, or shame. In secular society, "going all the way" means weaving only physically. "Going all the way" the Christian way means leaving, cleaving, and weaving spiritually, mentally, emotionally, physically, and faithfully with one spouse until parted by death. The former hurts and harms both people. The latter shows fear, love, and trust in God above all things and honors, loves, and cherishes the spouse. Whether we are married or single, all Christians are called to lead a sexually pure, decent life and to touch others with Christ's healing hands, honoring and keeping this delicate but delightful commandment.

After the Feast Comes the Reckoning

Proverbs doesn't deny the pull of sexual sin. It drips honey on the front end but is as bitter as wormwood on the back end.

> 5:1 My son, be attentive to my wisdom;
>
> incline your ear to my understanding,

2 that you may keep discretion,

>and your lips may guard knowledge.

3 For the lips of a forbidden woman drip honey,

>and her speech is smoother than oil,

4 but in the end she is bitter as wormwood,

>sharp as a two-edged sword.

5 Her feet go down to death;

>her steps follow the path to Sheol;

6 she does not ponder the path of life;

>her ways wander, and she does not know it.

7 And now, O sons, listen to me,

>and do not depart from the words of my mouth.

8 Keep your way far from her,

>and do not go near the door of her house,

9 lest you give your honor to others

>and your years to the merciless,

10 lest strangers take their fill of your strength,

>and your labors go to the house of a foreigner,

11 and at the end of your life you groan,

>when your flesh and body are consumed,

12 and you say, "How I hated discipline,

>and my heart despised reproof!

13 I did not listen to the voice of my teachers

>or incline my ear to my instructors.

14 I am at the brink of utter ruin

>in the assembled congregation."

Mark and Remark

Mark your favorite proverb above and remark why you chose it.

A Bird in the Hand Is Worth Two in the Bush

Pair and Share

3. Read 1 Corinthians 7:2–5. What's the wisdom of this passage?

God is not a killjoy; instead, God opposes what kills joy. Weaving physically before leaving and cleaving spiritually, mentally, and emotionally kills joy and creates shame. Even better, God proposes what creates joy: God created the first man and woman to be husband and wife, to have and to hold each other and to become one flesh together (Genesis 2:24). A husband and wife have nothing to be ashamed of when they are naked together (Genesis 2:25). What joy!

> 5:15 Drink water from your own cistern,
>> flowing water from your own well.
> 16 Should your springs be scattered abroad,
>> streams of water in the streets?
> 17 Let them be for yourself alone,
>> and not for strangers with you.
> 18 Let your fountain be blessed,
>> and rejoice in the wife of your youth,
> 19 a lovely deer, a graceful doe.
>> Let her breasts fill you at all times with delight;
>> be intoxicated always in her love.
> 20 Why should you be intoxicated, my son, with a forbidden woman
>> and embrace the bosom of an adulteress?

Mark and Remark

Mark your favorite proverb above and remark why you chose it.

Forbidden Fruit Is Sweet

"So when the woman saw that the tree was good for food, and that it was a delight to the eyes, and that the tree was to be desired to make one wise, she took of its fruit and ate, and she also gave some to her husband who was with her, and he ate" (Genesis 3:6). Ever since this first sin, original sin infects and defects us all with the same effect: our sinful nature sees the Law and seizes the opportunity to break it (Romans 7:7–12). After the fall, the fundamental flaw of the first use of the Law, the curb, is that it gives curb appeal to the forbidden. Forbidden fruit is sweet to our sinful nature. Since the following Sixth Commandment proverbs warn sons of the wiles of the forbidden woman, the adulteress, and the prostitute, so also should we warn daughters of the wiles of the philanderer, the sexual predator, and the sex trafficker.

7:1 My son, keep my words
and treasure up my commandments with you;

2 keep my commandments and live;
keep my teaching as the apple of your eye;

3 bind them on your fingers;
write them on the tablet of your heart.

4 Say to wisdom, "You are my sister,"
and call insight your intimate friend,

5 to keep you from the forbidden woman,
from the adulteress with her smooth words.

6 For at the window of my house
I have looked out through my lattice,

7 and I have seen among the simple,
I have perceived among the youths,
a young man lacking sense,

8 passing along the street near her corner,
taking the road to her house

9 in the twilight, in the evening,
at the time of night and darkness.

10 And behold, the woman meets him,
dressed as a prostitute, wily of heart.

11 She is loud and wayward;
her feet do not stay at home;

12 now in the street, now in the market,

and at every corner she lies in wait.

¹³ She seizes him and kisses him,

and with bold face she says to him,

¹⁴ "I had to offer sacrifices,

and today I have paid my vows;

¹⁵ so now I have come out to meet you,

to seek you eagerly, and I have found you.

¹⁶ I have spread my couch with coverings,

colored linens from Egyptian linen;

¹⁷ I have perfumed my bed with myrrh,

aloes, and cinnamon.

¹⁸ Come, let us take our fill of love till morning;

let us delight ourselves with love.

¹⁹ For my husband is not at home;

he has gone on a long journey;

²⁰ he took a bag of money with him;

at full moon he will come home."

²¹ With much seductive speech she persuades him;

with her smooth talk she compels him.

²² All at once he follows her,

as an ox goes to the slaughter,

or as a stag is caught fast

²³ till an arrow pierces its liver;

as a bird rushes into a snare;

he does not know that it will cost him his life.

²⁴ And now, O sons, listen to me,

and be attentive to the words of my mouth.

²⁵ Let not your heart turn aside to her ways;

do not stray into her paths,

²⁶ for many a victim has she laid low,

and all her slain are a mighty throng.

²⁷ Her house is the way to Sheol,

going down to the chambers of death.

⁹:¹³ The woman Folly is loud;

she is seductive and knows nothing.

¹⁴ She sits at the door of her house;

she takes a seat on the highest places of the town,

¹⁵ calling to those who pass by,

who are going straight on their way,

¹⁶ "Whoever is simple, let him turn in here!"

And to him who lacks sense she says,

¹⁷ "Stolen water is sweet,

and bread eaten in secret is pleasant."

¹⁸ But he does not know that the dead are there,

that her guests are in the depths of Sheol.

^{22:14} The mouth of forbidden women is a deep pit;

he with whom the LORD is angry will fall into it.

^{23:26} My son, give me your heart,

and let your eyes observe my ways.

²⁷ For a prostitute is a deep pit;

an adulteress is a narrow well.

²⁸ She lies in wait like a robber

and increases the traitors among mankind.

^{29:3} He who loves wisdom makes his father glad,

but a companion of prostitutes squanders his wealth.

Mark and Remark

Mark your favorite proverb above and remark why you chose it.

The Grass Is Always Greener on the Other Side

"It happened, late one afternoon, when David arose from his couch and was walking on the roof of the king's house, that he saw from the roof a woman bathing; and the woman was very beautiful" (2 Samuel 11:2). Even a man after God's own heart (1 Kings 11:4) can open his eyes to sin and harden his heart to God.

6:20 My son, keep your father's commandment,
and forsake not your mother's teaching.

21 Bind them on your heart always;
tie them around your neck.

22 When you walk, they will lead you;
when you lie down, they will watch over you;
and when you awake, they will talk with you.

23 For the commandment is a lamp and the teaching a light,
and the reproofs of discipline are the way of life,

24 to preserve you from the evil woman,
from the smooth tongue of the adulteress.

25 Do not desire her beauty in your heart,
and do not let her capture you with her eyelashes;

26 for the price of a prostitute is only a loaf of bread,
but a married woman hunts down a precious life.

27 Can a man carry fire next to his chest
and his clothes not be burned?

28 Or can one walk on hot coals
and his feet not be scorched?

29 So is he who goes in to his neighbor's wife;
none who touches her will go unpunished.

6:32 He who commits adultery lacks sense;
he who does it destroys himself.

33 He will get wounds and dishonor,
and his disgrace will not be wiped away.

11:22 Like a gold ring in a pig's snout
is a beautiful woman without discretion.

27:8 Like a bird that strays from its nest
is a man who strays from his home.

27:20 Sheol and Abaddon are never satisfied,
and never satisfied are the eyes of man.

Mark your favorite proverb above and remark why you chose it.

Marry in Haste, Repent in Leisure

In the Book of Proverbs, only one malady makes a marriage bad for a man. See the proverbs below. Two medicines make it better. Penultimately, Tommy and Tammy should show and tell each other that they honor, love, and cherish each other. Ultimately, Tommy and Tammy should practice peace and patience with each other's imperfections because they are forgiven, loved, and treasured by the perfect Father, Son, and Holy Spirit first.

19:13 A foolish son is ruin to his father,

and a wife's quarreling is a continual dripping of rain.

21:9 It is better to live in a corner of the housetop

than in a house shared with a quarrelsome wife.

21:19 It is better to live in a desert land

than with a quarrelsome and fretful woman.

25:24 It is better to live in a corner of the housetop

than in a house shared with a quarrelsome wife.[1]

27:15 A continual dripping on a rainy day

and a quarrelsome wife are alike;

16 to restrain her is to restrain the wind

or to grasp oil in one's right hand.

Mark your favorite proverb above and remark why you chose it.

---

1   Yes, Proverbs repeats itself word for word at 21:9 and 25:24.

It Takes Two to Tango

For better, for worse, no marriage is perfect. Sometimes our marriages look like that of Isaac and Rebekah. In Genesis 24, Isaac and Rebekah are a match made in heaven: "Then Isaac brought her into the tent of Sarah his mother and took Rebekah, and she became his wife, and he loved her" (Genesis 24:67). Only three chapters later, Rebekah deceives Isaac, dressing up one son, Jacob, to seem like the other son, Esau (Genesis 27:5–17). For Isaac and Rebekah and for us, marriage is for better, for worse, for richer, for poorer, in sickness and in health—the same way that Christ loves the Church.

12:4 An excellent wife is the crown of her husband,
  but she who brings shame is like rottenness in his bones.

14:1 The wisest of women builds her house,
  but folly with her own hands tears it down.

18:22 He who finds a wife finds a good thing
  and obtains favor from the LORD.

19:14 House and wealth are inherited from fathers,
  but a prudent wife is from the LORD.

Mark and Remark

Mark your favorite proverb above and remark why you chose it.

Personalize and Memorize

"Lead a sexually pure and decent life." With the Holy Spirit's help (John 14:26; Romans 8:11), keeping the Sixth Commandment means honoring God's plan for marriage by leaving, cleaving, and weaving spiritually, mentally, emotionally, and physically with one spouse until death parts the two of you. Analyze all the Sixth Commandment proverbs you previously marked and choose your favorite. Which proverb will help you keep the Sixth Commandment with fear, love, and trust because you are baptized—

because you are created in Christ—because God the Father forgives, loves, and treasures you in His Son first? Memorize it. Imagine a moment this week when you'll utilize your proverb. It will be pleasant if you keep it within you, if it is always ready on your lips (Proverbs 22:18).

Holy Lord, You instituted marriage in Eden, and by Your Word You uphold and protect this blessed union of man and woman in one flesh. Cause us to honor marriage and put away from us all sinful thoughts, words, and deeds that would dishonor and distort the gift of marriage. Bless all married couples with faithfulness. Hear the prayers of all who seek a godly spouse, and give to us all purity and decency in all things; through Jesus Christ, our Lord. Amen.[2]

---

2   *Luther's Small Catechism with Explanation,* Sixth Commandment, prayer.

CHAPTER 7

THE SEVENTH COMMANDMENT

You shall not steal. *What does this mean?* We should fear and love God so that we do not take our neighbor's money or possessions, or get them in any dishonest way, but help him to improve and protect his possessions and income.

Deep Memory

Dig deep and ink your First through Sixth Commandment proverbs.

Hippie or HIPPI?

Pair and Share

1. Imagine a hippie from the 1960s. What are three characteristics that come to mind?

Popular for breaking the Fourth Commandment, hippies in the 1960s were countercultural. They despised their parents and other authorities, preferring to huddle up and cuddle up with sex, drugs, and rock 'n' roll. When Luther explains the Seventh Commandment, he describes a different kind of hippie—*HIPPI:* "We should fear and love God so that we do not take our neighbor's money or possessions, or get them in any dishonest way, but *help* him to *improve* and *protect* his *possessions* and *income*" (emphasis added). Because of God's grace, a HIPPI is gracious to give, not greedy to get. These HIPPIs honor, love, and cherish their neighbor because God forgives, loves, and treasures them first. Who's more countercultural, a hippie or a HIPPI?

Lie Down with Dogs, Wake Up with Fleas

"A man was going down from Jerusalem to Jericho, and he fell among robbers, who stripped him and beat him and departed, leaving him half dead" (Luke 10:30). How does a man who begins life as a helpless little baby grow up to run with a ruthless pack of robbers? By hanging out with the wrong crowd. Keeping the Seventh Commandment begins by keeping away from junkyard dogs. When we do come close, we follow Jesus' example. Jesus ate with tax collectors and sinners not to join them but to better them—to seek and to save the lost (Luke 19:7–10).

> 1:8 Hear, my son, your father's instruction,
>> and forsake not your mother's teaching,
> 9 for they are a graceful garland for your head
>> and pendants for your neck.
> 10 My son, if sinners entice you,
>> do not consent.
> 11 If they say, "Come with us, let us lie in wait for blood;
>> let us ambush the innocent without reason;
> 12 like Sheol let us swallow them alive,
>> and whole, like those who go down to the pit;
> 13 we shall find all precious goods,
>> we shall fill our houses with plunder;
> 14 throw in your lot among us;
>> we will all have one purse"—
> 15 my son, do not walk in the way with them;
>> hold back your foot from their paths,
> 16 for their feet run to evil,
>> and they make haste to shed blood.
> 17 For in vain is a net spread
>> in the sight of any bird,
> 18 but these men lie in wait for their own blood;
>> they set an ambush for their own lives.

¹⁹ Such are the ways of everyone who is greedy for unjust gain;

it takes away the life of its possessors.

29:24 The partner of a thief hates his own life;

he hears the curse, but discloses nothing.

Mark and Remark

Mark your favorite proverb above and remark why you chose it.

Money Isn't Everything

Pair and Share

2. "Eat, drink, and be merry." What would you say to someone who lives by this motto? Read Luke 12:13–21 and answer this question.

God is not afraid to use fear to help free us from the false gods we fear, love, and trust more than Him—like money. French philosopher Blaise Pascal proposed his famous wager to provoke an appropriate fear of God: if you do not believe in God and God does not exist, what do you get? A little life where pleasure is the measure of all things. If you believe in God, but God does not exist, what do you get? A little life where you lose little. But if God exists and you believe in Him, you gain everything (John 3:18a). And if God exists and you do not believe in Him, you lose everything (John 3:18b). Money isn't everything.

11:4 Riches do not profit in the day of wrath,

but righteousness delivers from death.

11:7 When the wicked dies, his hope will perish,

and the expectation of wealth perishes too.

11:28 Whoever trusts in his riches will fall,

    but the righteous will flourish like a green leaf.

13:7 One pretends to be rich, yet has nothing;

    another pretends to be poor, yet has great wealth.

15:16 Better is a little with the fear of the LORD

    than great treasure and trouble with it.

17 Better is a dinner of herbs where love is

    than a fattened ox and hatred with it.

16:8 Better is a little with righteousness

    than great revenues with injustice.

16:19 It is better to be of a lowly spirit with the poor

    than to divide the spoil with the proud.

19:1 Better is a poor person who walks in his integrity

    than one who is crooked in speech and is a fool.

19:10 It is not fitting for a fool to live in luxury,

    much less for a slave to rule over princes.

19:22 What is desired in a man is steadfast love,

    and a poor man is better than a liar.

20:17 Bread gained by deceit is sweet to a man,

    but afterward his mouth will be full of gravel.

22:1 A good name is to be chosen rather than great riches,

    and favor is better than silver or gold.

28:6 Better is a poor man who walks in his integrity

    than a rich man who is crooked in his ways.

28:11 A rich man is wise in his own eyes,

    but a poor man who has understanding will find him out.

Mark and Remark

Mark your favorite proverb above and remark why you chose it.

Another Day, Another Dollar

Paul puts it right on the money: since you have been saved by grace (Ephesians 2:8), "let the thief no longer steal, but rather let him labor, doing honest work with his own hands, so that he may have something to share with anyone in need" (Ephesians 4:28). Keeping the Seventh Commandment means not only not stealing but also, day in and day out, doing an honest day's work with the Holy Spirit's help (Ephesians 4:30).

10:2 Treasures gained by wickedness do not profit,
> but righteousness delivers from death.

10:4 A slack hand causes poverty,
> but the hand of the diligent makes rich.

10:16 The wage of the righteous leads to life,
> the gain of the wicked to sin.

11:1 A false balance is an abomination to the LORD,
> but a just weight is His delight.[1]

11:18 The wicked earns deceptive wages,
> but one who sows righteousness gets a sure reward.

12:27 Whoever is slothful will not roast his game,
> but the diligent man will get precious wealth.

13:11 Wealth gained hastily will dwindle,
> but whoever gathers little by little will increase it.

14:24 The crown of the wise is their wealth,
> but the folly of fools brings folly.

---

1   How much more would you pay for a pound of bananas at the grocery store if the scales were off?

15:27 Whoever is greedy for unjust gain troubles his own household,

but he who hates bribes will live.

16:11 A just balance and scales are the LORD's;

all the weights in the bag are His work.

17:8 A bribe is like a magic stone in the eyes of the one who gives it;

wherever he turns he prospers.[2]

17:23 The wicked accepts a bribe in secret

to pervert the ways of justice.

17:26 To impose a fine on a righteous man is not good,

nor to strike the noble for their uprightness.

20:10 Unequal weights and unequal measures

are both alike an abomination to the LORD.

20:21 An inheritance gained hastily in the beginning

will not be blessed in the end.

20:23 Unequal weights are an abomination to the LORD,

and false scales are not good.

21:6 The getting of treasures by a lying tongue

is a fleeting vapor and a snare of death.

21:14 A gift in secret averts anger,

and a concealed bribe, strong wrath.[3]

23:4 Do not toil to acquire wealth;

be discerning enough to desist.

5 When your eyes light on it, it is gone,

for suddenly it sprouts wings,

flying like an eagle toward heaven.

28:20 A faithful man will abound with blessings,

but whoever hastens to be rich will not go unpunished.

21 To show partiality is not good,

---

2   A general rule that bribes do work like magic for the wicked.
3   A general rule that hush money does hush the wicked.

but for a piece of bread a man will do wrong.

22 A stingy man hastens after wealth

and does not know that poverty will come upon him.

28:25 A greedy man stirs up strife,

but the one who trusts in the LORD will be enriched.

Mark and Remark

Mark your favorite proverb above and remark why you chose it.

Eat to Live, Not Live to Eat

"Therefore do not be anxious, saying, 'What shall we eat?' or 'What shall we drink?' or 'What shall we wear?' For the Gentiles seek after all these things, and your heavenly Father knows that you need them all. But seek first the kingdom of God and His righteousness, and all these things will be added to you" (Matthew 6:31–33). Because your heavenly Father forgives, loves, and treasures you first, you can have confidence in the providence of God, a confidence that keeps the Seventh Commandment.

13:25 The righteous has enough to satisfy his appetite,

but the belly of the wicked suffers want.

21:17 Whoever loves pleasure will be a poor man;

he who loves wine and oil will not be rich.

21:20 Precious treasure and oil are in a wise man's dwelling,

but a foolish man devours it.

23:1 When you sit down to eat with a ruler,

observe carefully what is before you,

2 and put a knife to your throat

if you are given to appetite.

3 Do not desire his delicacies,

for they are deceptive food.

23:6 Do not eat the bread of a man who is stingy;

do not desire his delicacies,

7 for he is like one who is inwardly calculating.

"Eat and drink!" he says to you,

but his heart is not with you.

8 You will vomit up the morsels that you have eaten,

and waste your pleasant words.

23:19 Hear, my son, and be wise,

and direct your heart in the way.

20 Be not among drunkards

or among gluttonous eaters of meat,

21 for the drunkard and the glutton will come to poverty,

and slumber will clothe them with rags.

25:16 If you have found honey, eat only enough for you,

lest you have your fill of it and vomit it.

30:7 Two things I ask of You;

deny them not to me before I die:

8 Remove far from me falsehood and lying;

give me neither poverty nor riches;

feed me with the food that is needful for me,

9 lest I be full and deny You

and say, "Who is the LORD?"

or lest I be poor and steal

and profane the name of my God.

Mark and Remark

Mark your favorite proverb above and remark why you chose it.

Put Your Money Where Your Mouth Is

Pair and Share

3. Read Genesis 28:20–22. How do you put your money where your mouth is?

God's Word warns, "Beware lest you say in your heart, 'My power and the might of my hand have gotten me this wealth.' You shall remember the LORD . . . for it is He who gives you power to get wealth" (Deuteronomy 8:17–18). Because God gives me all that I need to support this body and life, honoring the Lord with my wealth is one way to test my confidence in God's providence.

> 3:9 Honor the LORD with your wealth
>> and with the firstfruits of all your produce;
> 10 then your barns will be filled with plenty,
>> and your vats will be bursting with wine.[4]

The Rich Get Richer and the Poor Get Poorer

Because God richly and daily provides us with all that we need to support this body and life, the Seventh Commandment commands us to help our neighbors improve and protect their possessions and income. The Book of Proverbs doesn't deny that this commandment gets broken. When it comes to general truths about the rich and the poor, the Book of Proverbs pulls no punches—and sometimes the truth hurts, especially if I am poor.

> 10:15 A rich man's wealth is his strong city;
>> the poverty of the poor is their ruin.

> 13:23 The fallow ground of the poor would yield much food,
>> but it is swept away through injustice.

> 14:20 The poor is disliked even by his neighbor,
>> but the rich has many friends.

---

4   There are always exceptions to general rules. Luther counsels, "Just do what is your duty. Let God manage how He will support you and provide enough for you" (Large Catechism I 165).

18:11 A rich man's wealth is his strong city,

and like a high wall in his imagination.

18:16 A man's gift makes room for him

and brings him before the great.

18:23 The poor use entreaties,

but the rich answer roughly.

19:4 Wealth brings many new friends,

but a poor man is deserted by his friend.

19:6 Many seek the favor of a generous man,

and everyone is a friend to a man who gives gifts.

7 All a poor man's brothers hate him;

how much more do his friends go far from him!

He pursues them with words, but does not have them.

22:7 The rich rules over the poor,

and the borrower is the slave of the lender.

28:3 A poor man who oppresses the poor

is a beating rain that leaves no food.

Mark and Remark

Mark your favorite proverb above and remark why you chose it.

Give Me Your Tired, Your Poor

When the world wants to talk about how awesome it is, it boasts about its wisdom and wealth, its beauty and health. But when God talks about how awesome He is, He boasts in His love for the least and the very vulnerable: "The LORD your God is God of gods and Lord of lords, the great, the mighty, and the awesome God, who is not partial and takes no bribe. He executes justice for the fatherless and the widow, and loves the sojourner, giving him food and clothing" (Deuteronomy 10:17–18).

Think and Ink

4. Peruse the proverbs below. What levels the playing field for the rich and the poor?

14:31 Whoever oppresses a poor man insults his Maker,

but he who is generous to the needy honors Him.

17:5 Whoever mocks the poor insults his Maker;

he who is glad at calamity will not go unpunished.

22:2 The rich and the poor meet together;

the LORD is the Maker of them all.

29:7 A righteous man knows the rights of the poor;

a wicked man does not understand such knowledge.

29:13 The poor man and the oppressor meet together;

the LORD gives light to the eyes of both.

31:8 Open your mouth for the mute,

for the rights of all who are destitute.

9 Open your mouth, judge righteously,

defend the rights of the poor and needy.

Mark and Remark

Mark your favorite proverb above and remark why you chose it.

What's Good for the Goose Is Good for the Gander

What if you had been in Bethlehem when poor baby Jesus had to hit the hay in a manger "because there was no place for them in the inn" (Luke 2:7)? Luther preaches:

> Many . . . are enkindled with dreamy devotion when they hear of this poverty of Christ; are almost angry with the citizens of Bethlehem, denounce their blindness and ingratitude; and think, if they had been there, they would have served the Lord and His mother and would not have let them be so miserable. But they do not look next door to see how many of their neighbors need their help, whom they ignore and leave as they are. Who is there on earth who has no poor, miserable, sick, erring, or sinful people around him? Why does he not exercise love to them? Why does he not do for them as Christ has done for him? It is untrue and false to think that you would have done much good for Christ, if you do nothing for them. If you had been at Bethlehem, you would have paid as little attention to Him as the others did.[5]

Jesus gives us a gander: when we love the least, feed the hungry, quench the thirsty, clothe the naked, visit the sick and those in prison, we are loving Him (Matthew 25:31–40). What's good for the goose is good for the gander.

3:27 Do not withhold good from those to whom it is due,

    when it is in your power to do it.

28 Do not say to your neighbor, "Go, and come again,

    tomorrow I will give it"—when you have it with you.

11:26 The people curse him who holds back grain,

    but a blessing is on the head of him who sells it.

13:22 A good man leaves an inheritance to his children's children,

    but the sinner's wealth is laid up for the righteous.

25:14 Like clouds and wind without rain

    is a man who boasts of a gift he does not give.

---

5   *Luther's Works*: American Edition, volume 75 (St. Louis: Concordia Publishing House, 2013), pages 224–25.

Mark and Remark

Mark your favorite proverb above and remark why you chose it.

It's Better to Give Than to Receive

Every Christian likely has "the Gospel in a nutshell" memorized, John 3:16: "For God so loved the world, that He gave His only Son, that whoever believes in Him should not perish but have eternal life." Everyone should also memorize how the Gospel comes out of its shell, 1 John 3:16: "By this we know love, that He laid down His life for us, and we ought to lay down our lives for the brothers." Because God forgives, loves, and treasures us first, we can honor, love, and cherish our neighbor with our treasures second.

11:24 One gives freely, yet grows all the richer;

another withholds what he should give, and only suffers want.

25 Whoever brings blessing will be enriched,

and one who waters will himself be watered.

14:21 Whoever despises his neighbor is a sinner,

but blessed is he who is generous to the poor.

19:17 Whoever is generous to the poor lends to the LORD,

and He will repay him for his deed.

22:9 Whoever has a bountiful eye will be blessed,

for he shares his bread with the poor.

28:27 Whoever gives to the poor will not want,

but he who hides his eyes will get many a curse.

Mark and Remark

Mark your favorite proverb above and remark why you chose it.

What Goes Around Comes Around

Keeping the Seventh Commandment means not only not stealing but also being a forgiven, loved, and treasured HIPPI who *helps* your neighbors *improve* and *protect* their *possessions* and *income*. Graced by God, a HIPPI is gracious to give, not greedy to get.

Pair and Share

5. Read Luke 16:19–26. What's the moral of this story?

21:13 Whoever closes his ear to the cry of the poor

will himself call out and not be answered.

22:16 Whoever oppresses the poor to increase his own wealth,

or gives to the rich, will only come to poverty.

22:22 Do not rob the poor, because he is poor,

or crush the afflicted at the gate,

23 for the LORD will plead their cause

and rob of life those who rob them.

Mark and Remark

Mark your favorite proverb above and remark why you chose it.

Personalize and Memorize

"Help him to improve and protect his possessions and income." With the Holy Spirit's help (John 14:26; Romans 8:11), keeping the Seventh Commandment means being a HIPPI—gracious to give, not greedy to get. Analyze all the Seventh Commandment proverbs you previously marked and choose your favorite. Which proverb will help you keep the Seventh Commandment with fear, love, and trust because you are baptized—because you are created in Christ—because God the Father forgives, loves, and treasures you in His Son first? Memorize it. Imagine a moment this week when you'll utilize your proverb. It will be pleasant if you keep it within you, if it is always ready on your lips (Proverbs 22:18).

Lord God, giver of every good and perfect gift, teach us to rejoice in the bounty of Your gifts given to our neighbors and curb our appetite to claim for ourselves by theft or dishonesty the money or possessions You have bestowed on them. Instead, give us cheerful hearts and willing hands to help our neighbors improve and protect their livelihood; through Jesus Christ, our Lord. Amen.[6]

---

6   *Luther's Small Catechism with Explanation*, Seventh Commandment, prayer.

CHAPTER 8

THE EIGHTH COMMANDMENT

You shall not give false testimony against your neighbor. *What does this mean?* We should fear and love God so that we do not tell lies about our neighbor, betray him, slander him, or hurt his reputation, but defend him, speak well of him, and explain everything in the kindest way.

Deep Memory

Dig deep and ink your First through Seventh Commandment proverbs.

Sitting in the Seat of Scoffers

Psalm 1 says, "Blessed is the man who walks not in the counsel of the wicked, nor stands in the way of sinners, nor sits in the seat of scoffers" (v. 1).

Pair and Share

1. We scarcely use the word *scoffer* now, but scoffing is scattered everywhere today. What is a scoffer? Google it.

2. How does Proverbs 21:24 define a scoffer?

There's an old German word for scoffing: *Schadenfreude*. *Schaden* means "misfortune," and *freude* means "delight." That's what scoffing is: to delight in someone else's misfortune.

Whenever I'm driving to work and I tune in to talk radio or NPR and I gloat, "*What!* That person did *that*?"—that's sitting in the seat of scoffers. Whenever I'm sitting in the cafeteria with my colleagues and I'm pointing out the imperfections of other people at work, that's sitting in the seat of scoffers. Whenever I'm on the internet and I delight myself in the misfortunes of the most popular, and then I scroll down to the comments and delight myself in the mindless, cold-hearted comments of modern-day scoffers, that's sitting in the seat of scoffers.

Psalm 1 says, "Don't get too comfortable sitting in the seat of scoffers." "[They] are like chaff that the wind drives away" (v. 4). They are like corn cobs that a combine leaves behind in the dirt. No flavor, no nutrition, not a kernel of wisdom in them. Like corn stalks on the day of harvest, scoffers "will not stand in the judgment" (v. 5).

"Blessed is the man who walks not in the counsel of the wicked, nor stands in the way of sinners, nor sits in the seat of scoffers" (v. 1); instead, "his delight is in the law of the LORD, and on His law he meditates day and night" (v. 2). Instead of scarring our neighbor with our scoffing, we can use the Eighth Commandment to meditate on how God has forgiven, loved, and treasured us with His Word (John 5:24) so that we may honor, love, and cherish our neighbor with our words.

A Lie Can Go around the World and Back Again While the Truth Is Lacing Up Its Boots

Think and Ink

3. Have you ever been the victim of someone's lie? Or worse, have you ever victimized someone with a lie? What happened?

The news is full of stories about wildfires all over the planet. The fires spread fast, and it always takes weeks or months to put them out. James compares, "How great a forest is set ablaze by such a small fire! And the tongue is a fire, a world of unrighteousness" (James 3:5–6).

10:18 The one who conceals hatred has lying lips,

and whoever utters slander is a fool.

13:17 A wicked messenger falls into trouble,

but a faithful envoy brings healing.

16:28 A dishonest man spreads strife,

and a whisperer separates close friends.

17:4 An evildoer listens to wicked lips,

and a liar gives ear to a mischievous tongue.

18:8 The words of a whisperer are like delicious morsels;

they go down into the inner parts of the body.

19:28 A worthless witness mocks at justice,

and the mouth of the wicked devours iniquity.

21:6 The getting of treasures by a lying tongue

is a fleeting vapor and a snare of death.

25:18 A man who bears false witness against his neighbor

is like a war club, or a sword, or a sharp arrow.

26:18 Like a madman who throws firebrands, arrows, and death

19 is the man who deceives his neighbor

and says, "I am only joking!"

26:24 Whoever hates disguises himself with his lips

and harbors deceit in his heart;

25 when he speaks graciously, believe him not,

for there are seven abominations in his heart;

26 though his hatred be covered with deception,

his wickedness will be exposed in the assembly.

26:28 A lying tongue hates its victims,

and a flattering mouth works ruin.

Mark and Remark

Mark your favorite proverb above and remark why you chose it.

The Truth Will Come Out

Yes, wildfires spread fast, but painfully and patiently, they always go out. Yes, lies spread like wildfire, but painfully and patiently, the truth will come out. On the night Jesus was betrayed, "many bore false witness against Him" (Mark 14:56). But painfully and patiently, three days later, the Truth came out of the tomb (Mark 16:6). The truth will come out.

Think and Ink

4. Honesty is the best policy. True or false? Read Exodus 1:15–20 and answer this question.

12:17 Whoever speaks the truth gives honest evidence,

but a false witness utters deceit.

14:5 A faithful witness does not lie,

but a false witness breathes out lies.

14:25 A truthful witness saves lives,

but one who breathes out lies is deceitful.

19:5 A false witness will not go unpunished,

and he who breathes out lies will not escape.

19:9 A false witness will not go unpunished,

and he who breathes out lies will perish.

20:5 The purpose in a man's heart is like deep water,

but a man of understanding will draw it out.[1]

21:28 A false witness will perish,

but the word of a man who hears will endure.

24:28 Be not a witness against your neighbor without cause,

and do not deceive with your lips.

Mark and Remark

Mark your favorite proverb above and remark why you chose it.

Evil to Him Who Thinks Evil

Hurting our neighbor's reputation to help our reputation breaks the Eighth Commandment. Luther denounces this standard double standard:

It is a common evil plague that everyone prefers hearing evil more than hearing good about his neighbor. We ourselves are so bad that we cannot allow anyone to say anything bad about us. Everyone

---

1   At Luke 20:1–8, Jesus answers a question with a question to expose duplicity.

would much prefer that all the world should speak of him in glowing terms. Yet we cannot bear that the best is spoken about others.[2]

1:22 How long, O simple ones, will you love being simple?

How long will scoffers delight in their scoffing

and fools hate knowledge?

6:12 A worthless person, a wicked man,

goes about with crooked speech,

13 winks with his eyes, signals with his feet,

points with his finger,

14 with perverted heart devises evil,

continually sowing discord;

15 therefore calamity will come upon him suddenly;

in a moment he will be broken beyond healing.

9:7 Whoever corrects a scoffer gets himself abuse,

and he who reproves a wicked man incurs injury.

8 Do not reprove a scoffer, or he will hate you;

reprove a wise man, and he will love you.

10:10 Whoever winks the eye causes trouble,

and a babbling fool will come to ruin.

10:14 The wise lay up knowledge,

but the mouth of a fool brings ruin near.

11:13 Whoever goes about slandering reveals secrets,

but he who is trustworthy in spirit keeps a thing covered.

13:1 A wise son hears his father's instruction,

but a scoffer does not listen to rebuke.

14:6 A scoffer seeks wisdom in vain,

but knowledge is easy for a man of understanding.

7 Leave the presence of a fool,

for there you do not meet words of knowledge.

---

2   Large Catechism I 264.

15:12 A scoffer does not like to be reproved;

he will not go to the wise.

17:14 The beginning of strife is like letting out water,

so quit before the quarrel breaks out.

17:20 A man of crooked heart does not discover good,

and one with a dishonest tongue falls into calamity.

18:6 A fool's lips walk into a fight,

and his mouth invites a beating.

7 A fool's mouth is his ruin,

and his lips are a snare to his soul.

19:29 Condemnation is ready for scoffers,

and beating for the backs of fools.

20:19 Whoever goes about slandering reveals secrets;

therefore do not associate with a simple babbler.

21:11 When a scoffer is punished, the simple becomes wise;

when a wise man is instructed, he gains knowledge.

21:24 "Scoffer" is the name of the arrogant, haughty man

who acts with arrogant pride.

22:10 Drive out a scoffer, and strife will go out,

and quarreling and abuse will cease.

23:9 Do not speak in the hearing of a fool,

for he will despise the good sense of your words.

24:9 The devising of folly is sin,

and the scoffer is an abomination to mankind.

25:23 The north wind brings forth rain,

and a backbiting tongue, angry looks.

26:21 As charcoal to hot embers and wood to fire,

so is a quarrelsome man for kindling strife.

29:8 Scoffers set a city aflame,

but the wise turn away wrath.

Mark and Remark

Mark your favorite proverb above and remark why you chose it.

Look on the Bright Side

Because of God the Father's kindness toward us in Christ Jesus, the Eighth Commandment commands us to explain everything in the kindest way. When Nathanael first heard about Jesus, he presumed Jesus was a nobody from Nazareth (John 1:45–46), accenting the negative. But when Nathanael met Jesus, Jesus accented the positive: "Behold, an Israelite indeed, in whom there is no deceit" (John 1:47). Yes, Jesus knew what Nathanael said (John 1:48), but Jesus proceeded to give Nathanael His forgiveness and grace, quoting from Psalm 32:1–2: "Blessed is the one whose transgression is forgiven, whose sin is covered. Blessed is the man against whom the LORD counts no iniquity, and in whose spirit there is no deceit." Because Jesus Christ is the light of the world (John 8:12) who takes away the sin of world (John 1:29), Christians can always look on the bright side.

4:24 Put away from you crooked speech,

and put devious talk far from you.

10:12 Hatred stirs up strife,

but love covers all offenses.

16:13 Righteous lips are the delight of a king,

and he loves him who speaks what is right.

17:9 Whoever covers an offense seeks love,

but he who repeats a matter separates close friends.

17:27 Whoever restrains his words has knowledge,

and he who has a cool spirit is a man of understanding.

18:4 The words of a man's mouth are deep waters;

the fountain of wisdom is a bubbling brook.

19:11 Good sense makes one slow to anger,

and it is his glory to overlook an offense.

21:21 Whoever pursues righteousness and kindness

will find life, righteousness, and honor.

21:23 Whoever keeps his mouth and his tongue

keeps himself out of trouble.

Mark and Remark

Mark your favorite proverb above and remark why you chose it.

The Medium Is the Message

While there is nothing new under the sun, modern broadcast media and social media amplify our sinful love for the crude and rude. Because of this, more Christians are discovering the discipline of unplugging—unplugging from the media to plug into Christ. While the media are sometimes mean, Christ is always love: "Love is patient and kind; love does not envy or boast; it is not arrogant or rude. It does not insist on its own way; it is not irritable or resentful; it does not rejoice at wrongdoing, but rejoices with the truth" (1 Corinthians 13:4–6). When we're plugged into Christ, we Christians have the power to love our neighbor with our lips, keeping the Eighth Commandment.

10:11 The mouth of the righteous is a fountain of life,

but the mouth of the wicked conceals violence.

10:31 The mouth of the righteous brings forth wisdom,

but the perverse tongue will be cut off.

32 The lips of the righteous know what is acceptable,

but the mouth of the wicked, what is perverse.

11:9 With his mouth the godless man would destroy his neighbor,

but by knowledge the righteous are delivered.

11:17 A man who is kind benefits himself,

but a cruel man hurts himself.

12:5 The thoughts of the righteous are just;

the counsels of the wicked are deceitful.

6 The words of the wicked lie in wait for blood,

but the mouth of the upright delivers them.

12:13 An evil man is ensnared by the transgression of his lips,

but the righteous escapes from trouble.

12:16 The vexation of a fool is known at once,

but the prudent ignores an insult.

12:18 There is one whose rash words are like sword thrusts,

but the tongue of the wise brings healing.

19 Truthful lips endure forever,

but a lying tongue is but for a moment.

12:22 Lying lips are an abomination to the LORD,

but those who act faithfully are His delight.

13:17 A wicked messenger falls into trouble,

but a faithful envoy brings healing.

15:2 The tongue of the wise commends knowledge,

but the mouths of fools pour out folly.

15:7 The lips of the wise spread knowledge;

not so the hearts of fools.

28:10 Whoever misleads the upright into an evil way

will fall into his own pit,

but the blameless will have a goodly inheritance.

Mark and Remark

Mark your favorite proverb above and remark why you chose it.

Don't Air Dirty Laundry in Public

Oops! Christians accidentally break the Eighth Commandment by confusing Matthew 18:15 with Matthew 10:27. When Timmy sins against me, instead of going and telling it to him alone, I go and proclaim it on the housetops, telling it to the world: "Look at his dirty laundry!" It's the Gospel that's supposed to go out to the world, not Timmy's mess-ups.

Pair and Share

5. Read Matthew 18:15–20. What happens when we put steps 2 and 3 before step 1?

24:24 Whoever says to the wicked, "You are in the right,"
    will be cursed by peoples, abhorred by nations,
  25 but those who rebuke the wicked will have delight,
    and a good blessing will come upon them.

25:7 What your eyes have seen
  8 do not hastily bring into court,
    for what will you do in the end,
    when your neighbor puts you to shame?
  9 Argue your case with your neighbor himself,
    and do not reveal another's secret,
  10 lest he who hears you bring shame upon you,
    and your ill repute have no end.

Mark and Remark

Mark your favorite proverb above and remark why you chose it.

Words Once Spoken You Can Never Recall

Think and Ink

6. Loose lips sink ships. What's the worst thing you ever said that you wish you could recall?

"No memory burns" is a rule in our house: you shall not burn a bad memory in someone's memory with your bad words. All of us can recall something someone said about us, and all of us can recall something we said that we wish we could recall. Whenever we recall our past sins, let us also recall the distinction of Law and Gospel. The Law not only "teaches what is right and pleasing to God" but also "rebukes everything that is sin and contrary to God's will."[3] "But the Gospel is properly the kind of teaching that shows what a person who has not kept the Law . . . is to believe. It teaches that Christ has paid for and made satisfaction for all sins [Romans 5:9]. Christ has gained and acquired for an individual—without any of his own merit—forgiveness of sins, righteousness that avails before God, and eternal life [Romans 5:10]."[4] Whenever we recall words that we wish we could recall, let us recall the Word of God that He will never recall: "If we say we have no sin, we deceive ourselves, and the truth is not in us. If we confess our sins, He is faithful and just to forgive us our sins and to cleanse us from all unrighteousness" (1 John 1:8–9).

11:12 Whoever belittles his neighbor lacks sense,

but a man of understanding remains silent.

---

3   Epitome V 3.
4   Epitome V 5. Brackets in original.

16:27 A worthless man plots evil,

and his speech is like a scorching fire.

28 A dishonest man spreads strife,

and a whisperer separates close friends.

18:19 A brother offended is more unyielding than a strong city,

and quarreling is like the bars of a castle.

18:21 Death and life are in the power of the tongue,

and those who love it will eat its fruits.

20:25 It is a snare to say rashly, "It is holy,"

and to reflect only after making vows.

26:17 Whoever meddles in a quarrel not his own

is like one who takes a passing dog by the ears.

26:20 For lack of wood the fire goes out,

and where there is no whisperer, quarreling ceases.

29:11 A fool gives full vent to his spirit,

but a wise man quietly holds it back.

Mark and Remark

Mark your favorite proverb above and remark why you chose it.

Keep Your Mouth Shut and Your Ears Open

The Eighth Commandment commands honoring, loving, and cherishing our neighbor not only with our tongues but also with our ears. "Let every person be quick to hear, slow to speak, slow to anger; for the anger of man does not produce the righteousness of God" (James 1:19–20). Speech is silver; silence is golden.

12:23 A prudent man conceals knowledge,

but the heart of fools proclaims folly.

15:28 The heart of the righteous ponders how to answer,

but the mouth of the wicked pours out evil things.

16:21 The wise of heart is called discerning,

and sweetness of speech increases persuasiveness.

16:23 The heart of the wise makes his speech judicious

and adds persuasiveness to his lips.

17:27 Whoever restrains his words has knowledge,

and he who has a cool spirit is a man of understanding.

28 Even a fool who keeps silent is considered wise;

when he closes his lips, he is deemed intelligent.

18:2 A fool takes no pleasure in understanding,

but only in expressing his opinion.

18:13 If one gives an answer before he hears,

it is his folly and shame.

18:17 The one who states his case first seems right,

until the other comes and examines him.

20:3 It is an honor for a man to keep aloof from strife,

but every fool will be quarreling.

26:4 Answer not a fool according to his folly,

lest you be like him yourself.

29:20 Do you see a man who is hasty in his words?

There is more hope for a fool than for him.

Mark and Remark

Mark your favorite proverb above and remark why you chose it.

Less Is More

When the Pharisees found a woman caught in adultery, they had twenty-seven words to say: "Teacher, this woman has been caught in the act of adultery. Now in the Law, Moses commanded us to stone such women. So what do You say?" (John 8:4–5). When Jesus heard the pot calling the kettle black, He had only seventeen words to say: "Let him who is without sin among you be the first to throw a stone at her" (John 8:7). Less is more.

10:19 When words are many, transgression is not lacking,

but whoever restrains his lips is prudent.

12:14 From the fruit of his mouth a man is satisfied with good,

and the work of a man's hand comes back to him.

13:3 Whoever guards his mouth preserves his life;

he who opens wide his lips comes to ruin.

15:23 To make an apt answer is a joy to a man,

and a word in season, how good it is!

17:7 Fine speech is not becoming to a fool;

still less is false speech to a prince.

18:4 The words of a man's mouth are deep waters;

the fountain of wisdom is a bubbling brook.

18:20 From the fruit of a man's mouth his stomach is satisfied;

he is satisfied by the yield of his lips.

25:20 Whoever sings songs to a heavy heart

is like one who takes off a garment on a cold day,

and like vinegar on soda.

26:7 Like a lame man's legs, which hang useless,

is a proverb in the mouth of fools.

26:9 Like a thorn that goes up into the hand of a drunkard

is a proverb in the mouth of fools.

27:14 Whoever blesses his neighbor with a loud voice,

> rising early in the morning,
>
> will be counted as cursing.

29:9 If a wise man has an argument with a fool,

> the fool only rages and laughs, and there is no quiet.

Mark your favorite proverb above and remark why you chose it.

Honey Catches More Flies Than Vinegar

When Timmy lies about Tommy and I go and tell others what Timmy did, then I'm all fact and no tact. When Timmy lies about Tommy and I listen silently to Timmy's lies, I'm all tact and no fact. The Eighth Commandment commands a communion of fact and tact: "Brothers, if anyone is caught in any transgression, you who are spiritual should restore him in a spirit of gentleness" (Galatians 6:1). When Timmy lies about Tommy and you tell Timmy to forgive, love, and treasure Tommy because God forgives, loves, and treasures Timmy first, that communion of fact and tact keeps the Eighth Commandment.

10:20 The tongue of the righteous is choice silver;

> the heart of the wicked is of little worth.

21 The lips of the righteous feed many,

> but fools die for lack of sense.

12:25 Anxiety in a man's heart weighs him down,

> but a good word makes him glad.

15:1 A soft answer turns away wrath,

> but a harsh word stirs up anger.

15:4 A gentle tongue is a tree of life,

> but perverseness in it breaks the spirit.

16:24 Gracious words are like a honeycomb,

sweetness to the soul and health to the body.

22:11 He who loves purity of heart,

and whose speech is gracious, will have the king as his friend.

24:26 Whoever gives an honest answer

kisses the lips.

25:11 A word fitly spoken

is like apples of gold in a setting of silver.

25:15 With patience a ruler may be persuaded,

and a soft tongue will break a bone.

25:25 Like cold water to a thirsty soul,

so is good news from a far country.

Mark and Remark

Mark your favorite proverb above and remark why you chose it.

Flattery Will Get You Nowhere

"What are you giving up for Lent this year?" The Gospel for Ash Wednesday tells us not to flatter ourselves by answering this question:

> And when you fast, do not look gloomy like the hypocrites, for they disfigure their faces that their fasting may be seen by others. Truly, I say to you, they have received their reward. But when you fast, anoint your head and wash your face, that your fasting may not be seen by others but by your Father who is in secret. And your Father who sees in secret will reward you. (Matthew 6:16–18)

Common sense says, "Toot your own horn lest the same be never tooted," but the Bible says, "Do not let your left hand know what your right hand is doing" (Matthew 6:3). Flattery always falls flat.

25:27 It is not good to eat much honey,

nor is it glorious to seek one's own glory.

26:1 Like snow in summer or rain in harvest,

so honor is not fitting for a fool.

27:2 Let another praise you, and not your own mouth;

a stranger, and not your own lips.

27:6 Faithful are the wounds of a friend;

profuse are the kisses of an enemy.

27:21 The crucible is for silver, and the furnace is for gold,

and a man is tested by his praise.

28:23 Whoever rebukes a man will afterward find more favor

than he who flatters with his tongue.

29:5 A man who flatters his neighbor

spreads a net for his feet.

30:32 If you have been foolish, exalting yourself,

or if you have been devising evil,

put your hand on your mouth.

33 For pressing milk produces curds,

pressing the nose produces blood,

and pressing anger produces strife.

Mark and Remark

Mark your favorite proverb above and remark why you chose it.

Personalize and Memorize

"Defend him, speak well of him, and explain everything in the kindest way." With the Holy Spirit's help (John 14:26; Romans 8:11), keeping the Eighth Commandment means honoring, loving, and cherishing our neighbor with our words. Analyze all the Eighth Commandment proverbs you previously marked and choose your favorite. Which proverb will help you keep the Eighth Commandment with fear, love, and trust because you are baptized—because you are created in Christ—because God the Father forgives, loves, and treasures you in His Son first? Memorize it. Imagine a moment this week when you'll utilize your proverb. It will be pleasant if you keep it within you, if it is always ready on your lips (Proverbs 22:18).

Guard our lips, O Lord, and govern our unruly tongues so that our words about our neighbors are not tainted with falsehood, betrayal, or slander, which would damage their reputation. Instead, give us the wisdom to speak well of our neighbors, defend them, and explain their circumstances and actions in the kindest way; through Jesus Christ, our Lord. Amen.[5]

---

5   *Luther's Small Catechism with Explanation,* Eighth Commandment, prayer.

CHAPTER 9

THE NINTH COMMANDMENT

You shall not covet your neighbor's house. *What does this mean?* We should fear and love God so that we do not scheme to get our neighbor's inheritance or house, or get it in a way which only appears right, but help and be of service to him in keeping it.

Deep Memory

Dig deep and ink your First through Eighth Commandment proverbs.

From Holey to Holy

The Ninth and Tenth Commandments both command, "You shall not covet." These two commandments aren't merely the last in the list; their meanings mirror the First and foremost Commandment. If the First Commandment means fearing, loving, and trusting in God with our hearts, then the Ninth and Tenth Commandments mean guarding our hearts so that they can fear, love, and trust in God. Coveting is sinful desire—the unholy hurry in our holey hearts to get what God has not given. "What causes quarrels and what causes fights among you? Is it not this, that your passions are at war within you? You desire and do not have, so you murder. You covet and cannot obtain, so you fight and quarrel" (James 4:1–2). Because of coveting—because there are sinful desires in our hearts—there are also sinful words spoken on our lips and sinful actions committed with our hands.

Holey

In the beginning, God created a place for everything, even a place for Himself: first place. When God gets first place in our hearts, everything else falls into place. But when God comes in second, third, or last place, everything else falls out of place. Coveting happens when our hearts feel holey. Like a hole in your stomach that grumbles, a holey heart is a heart that hurts—a hole in your soul that longs to be filled. When my heart feels holey, that's when I covet, desiring to fill it up with a false god—fearing, loving, and trusting in a person, place, thing, or idea more than God, placing something in this creation in the place where only God is meant to go (Romans 1:25). God created everything in creation "very good" (Genesis 1:31), and everything created in creation remains very good when it is enjoyed as a good and perfect gift from an even greater Creator (James 1:17). But creation goes from very good to very bad when the gift is enjoyed more than the Giver. For example, God created wine, the fruit of the vine (Psalm 104:14–15), to be enjoyed as a good and perfect gift from an even greater Creator (1 Timothy 4:4–5), but vino goes from very good to very bad when the gift is enjoyed more than the Giver. Coveting exploits God's good creation, adulterating it into a little-g false god in place of the big-G true God. When our hearts feel holey, that's when we're most tempted to covet and submit to sin. As Augustine says in his Confessions, "Our hearts are restless until they rest in You."

Think and Ink

1. The popular acronym HALT stands for Hungry, Angry, Lonely, or Tired. When we're hungry, angry, lonely, or tired, that's when we stop at Temptation Station. (I would add that this acronym could also mean Hurried, Anxious, Lazy, or Touchy.) When do you feel most tempted to covet and submit to sin?

Holy

"We do not have a high priest who is unable to sympathize with our weaknesses, but one who in every respect has been tempted as we are, yet without sin" (Hebrews 4:15). In Matthew 4, when Jesus felt holey and hungry, He defeated the top three temptations, pleasure (4:1–4), pride (4:5–7), and power (4:8–11), with His Holy Word. Throughout His whole life, whenever Jesus felt holey, He remained holy, faithfully fulfilling what we fail to fulfill. For the sake of the joy of eternal fellowship with you and me, He fulfilled the Law in our place, paid our penalty in our place, and rose again to prepare a place for us in heaven. He became holey in His heart and holey His hands to make you and me holy.

After the Holy Spirit calls, gathers, and enlightens us with God the Father's grace in Jesus Christ, He immediately goes to work to sanctify us and guard our hearts (Philippians 4:4–7), moving our hearts from dissatisfaction to satisfaction, from coveting to contentment, from holey to holy. The Holy Spirit guards our hearts by helping us become grateful for all the ways God has been gracious to us (Colossians 3:17).

Pair and Share

2. What are five things you're thankful for today?

There are three kinds of gifts God the Father, Son, and Holy Spirit give to us. God the Father gives us First Article gifts as our Creator (Genesis 1 and 2), Provider (Matthew 5:43–48), and Father (Luke 15:11–24). First Article gifts include my body and soul, all the material things I need to support this body and life, and His fatherly discipline and love. God the Son gives us Second Article gifts as our Prophet (John 1:18), Priest (Hebrews 2:17), and King (1 Corinthians 15:55–57). Second Article gifts include the wisdom of His Word, His sacrifice for our sins, and His victory over sin, Satan, death, and hell. God the Holy Spirit gives us Third Article gifts as our Caller and Gatherer (John 15:26), Enlightener (1 Corinthians 2:6–16), and Sanctifier (Galatians 5:22–24). Third Article gifts include our conversion, our comprehension of spiritual wisdom, and the fruit of the Holy Spirit: love, joy, peace, patience, kindness, goodness, faithfulness, gentleness, and self-control. Everything we could ever ask for is either a First Article, Second Article, or Third Article gift!

Think and Ink

3. Review the five things you're thankful for today. Categorize each one. Is it a First Article, Second Article, or Third Article gift? What's insightful about categorizing the things you're thankful for?

With the Holy Spirit's help (Romans 8:11), keeping the Ninth Commandment means guarding our hearts, moving from coveting to counting to our blessings. When we're content with what God has given us, then we can help and be of service to our neighbors in keeping what God has given them.

Pair and Share

4. What would happen to your heart if every day (maybe on your way home from work or school), you thanked God the Father for one or two First Article gifts, God the Son for one or two Second Article gifts, and God the Holy Spirit for one or two Third Article gifts?

You Get What You Get, and You Don't Throw a Fit

A wise mentor at the seminary told us future pastors to always take our coffee black. Why? For two reasons: First, you don't want to look covetous and make your host do extra work, having to grab the cream and sugar for you. Second, dark, bitter brew reminds us of the blackness of our sins and our need for our Savior. Similarly, Paul tells us to find our fulfillment not in creature comforts but in Christ: "I have learned in whatever situation I am to be content. I know how to be brought low, and I know how to abound. In any and every circumstance, I have learned the secret of facing plenty and hunger, abundance and need. I can do all things through Him who strengthens me" (Philippians 4:11–13).

10:3 The LORD does not let the righteous go hungry,

but He thwarts the craving of the wicked.[1]

10:28 The hope of the righteous brings joy,

but the expectation of the wicked will perish.

11:6 The righteousness of the upright delivers them,

but the treacherous are taken captive by their lust.

11:23 The desire of the righteous ends only in good,

the expectation of the wicked in wrath.

11:27 Whoever diligently seeks good seeks favor,

but evil comes to him who searches for it.

12:12 Whoever is wicked covets the spoil of evildoers,

but the root of the righteous bears fruit.

13:25 The righteous has enough to satisfy his appetite,

but the belly of the wicked suffers want.

23:17 Let not your heart envy sinners,

but continue in the fear of the LORD all the day.

24:8 Whoever plans to do evil

will be called a schemer.

24:19 Fret not yourself because of evildoers,

and be not envious of the wicked,

20 for the evil man has no future;

the lamp of the wicked will be put out.

27:4 Wrath is cruel, anger is overwhelming,

but who can stand before jealousy?

27:7 One who is full loathes honey,

but to one who is hungry everything bitter is sweet.

30:15 Three things are never satisfied;

---

1   There are always exceptions to general rules. Luther again counsels, "Just do what is your duty. Let God manage how He will support you and provide enough for you" (Large Catechism I 165).

four never say, "Enough":

16 Sheol, the barren womb,

the land never satisfied with water,

and the fire that never says, "Enough."

Mark and Remark

Mark your favorite proverb above and remark why you chose it.

Look Before You Leap

Pair and Share

5. Discretion is the better part of valor. What was the hardest decision you have ever had to make? How did you finally decide?

Common sense says, "Don't put all your eggs in one basket." But Jesus Christ says, "Put all your eggs in My Easter basket." "If anyone would come after Me, let him deny himself and take up his cross and follow Me. For whoever would save his life will lose it, but whoever loses his life for My sake will find it" (Matthew 16:24–25). The cost of discipleship not only costs everything but is also worth everything.

14:8 The wisdom of the prudent is to discern his way,

but the folly of fools is deceiving.

14:15 The simple believes everything,

but the prudent gives thought to his steps.

16 One who is wise is cautious and turns away from evil,

but a fool is reckless and careless.

14:22 Do they not go astray who devise evil?

Those who devise good meet steadfast love and faithfulness.

16:17 The highway of the upright turns aside from evil;

whoever guards his way preserves his life.

21:29 A wicked man puts on a bold face,

but the upright gives thought to his ways.

22:3 The prudent sees danger and hides himself,

but the simple go on and suffer for it.

27:12 The prudent sees danger and hides himself,

but the simple go on and suffer for it.[2]

Mark and Remark

Mark your favorite proverb above and remark why you chose it.

Keep Your Eyes on the Prize

Haste makes waste. Coveting is always in a hurry. It wants *right now* what God has not given: "Their end is destruction, their god is their belly, and they glory in their shame, with minds set on earthly things" (Philippians 3:19). But God has got the very best for us at the end of a slow and steady race: "Our citizenship is in heaven, and from it we await a Savior, the Lord Jesus Christ, who will transform our lowly body to be like His glorious body, by the power that enables Him even to subject all things to Himself" (Philippians 3:20–21). Keeping the Ninth Commandment means keeping your eyes on the prize.

19:2 Desire without knowledge is not good,

and whoever makes haste with his feet misses his way.

21:5 The plans of the diligent lead surely to abundance,

but everyone who is hasty comes only to poverty.

---

2   Yes, Proverbs repeats itself word for word at 22:3 and 27:12.

Mark your favorite proverb above and remark why you chose it.

Dig the Well before You Are Thirsty

My students and I can sympathize with one another's sinful natures. So often on campus, we rest when we should be working and work when we should be resting. This imbalance of labor and leisure cuts a hole in our hearts with hurry, anxiety, laziness, and touchiness, causing us to covet immediate relief and submit to sin. We know God has written "business before pleasure" and "work before play" on our hearts (Romans 2:14–15), but none of us has the capacity to carry it out (Romans 7:18). Christ alone is righteous and has done everything at the right time, "for while we were still weak, at the right time Christ died for the ungodly" (Romans 5:6).

24:27 Prepare your work outside;

get everything ready for yourself in the field,

and after that build your house.

Good Fences Make Good Neighbors

6. Familiarity breeds contempt? Read Luke 11:5–13. How does Jesus encourage us to see our heavenly Father as much greater than a grumpy neighbor who doesn't want to be bothered?

Proverbs says, "Let your foot be seldom found in your neighbor's house," but let your foot be often found in your Father's house. You need not covet your neighbor's house, because Christ has a place for you in your Father's house (John 14:2).

25:17 Let your foot be seldom in your neighbor's house,

> lest he have his fill of you and hate you.

A Merry Heart Makes a Cheerful Countenance

"Turn that frown upside down." I frown when I'm down—when my plans don't go according to plan and my heart hurts. On days like these, the song I sing sounds like this:

> Oh, what a horrible morning,
>
> Oh, what a horrible day,
>
> I've got a really bad feeling,
>
> Nothing is going my way.

But no matter how many horrible mornings and horrible days happen, because of Christ's crucifixion and resurrection, God's got an unending, beautiful morning He's keeping in heaven for you (1 Peter 1:3–4). No matter how many horrible mornings and horrible days happen, *that* beautiful morning and *that* beautiful day is going to happen. In the meantime, God uses even horrible mornings and horrible days to strengthen our grip on the Gospel (1 Peter 1:6–7). How often I fear, love, and trust in beautiful mornings and beautiful days more than God! And God can loosen my namby-pamby grip on beautiful mornings and beautiful days only by allowing horrible mornings and horrible days to whap my fingers. "Beloved, do not be surprised at the fiery trial when it comes upon you to test you, as though something strange were happening to you. But rejoice insofar as you share Christ's sufferings, that you may also rejoice and be glad when His glory is revealed" (1 Peter 4:12–13). God's Word can turn the song we sing around:

> Oh, what a horrible morning,
>
> Oh, what a horrible day,
>
> But I've got a wonderful feeling,
>
> Everything's going God's way.
>
> Turn that frown upside down!

13:12 Hope deferred makes the heart sick,

> but a desire fulfilled is a tree of life.

13:19 A desire fulfilled is sweet to the soul,

but to turn away from evil is an abomination to fools.

14:10 The heart knows its own bitterness,

and no stranger shares its joy.

14:13 Even in laughter the heart may ache,

and the end of joy may be grief.

14:30 A tranquil heart gives life to the flesh,

but envy makes the bones rot.

15:13 A glad heart makes a cheerful face,

but by sorrow of heart the spirit is crushed.

15:15 All the days of the afflicted are evil,

but the cheerful of heart has a continual feast.

15:30 The light of the eyes rejoices the heart,

and good news refreshes the bones.

17:22 A joyful heart is good medicine,

but a crushed spirit dries up the bones.

18:14 A man's spirit will endure sickness,

but a crushed spirit who can bear?

27:19 As in water face reflects face,

so the heart of man reflects the man.

Mark and Remark

Mark your favorite proverb above and remark why you chose it.

Guard Your Heart

Penultimately, the Holy Spirit helps us guard our hearts with the Ninth Commandment, moving us from coveting to contentment. But our Old Adam is not content to count his blessings; our sinful nature's nature is to keep on coveting.[3] So we cannot ultimately guard our hearts with how well we keep the Ninth Commandment. Ultimately, the Holy Spirit must guard our hearts with the Gospel. Jesus calls the Holy Spirit the Helper (*Paraklete* in Greek; John 15:26). I ask my student-athletes, "Do you wear a pair of loafers or a pair of cleats when you play your sport on the turf?" They wear a pair of cleats to get a grip on the ground. If they wore a pair of loafers, they'd be slip-sliding away. In the same way, the Holy Spirit (the *Paraklete*) is like a pair of cleats. When we're slip-sliding away in our weakness and covetous sin, the Holy Spirit guards our hearts and grounds our feet in the Gospel: God the Father forgives, loves, and treasures you in His Son, Jesus Christ. "It is finished" (John 19:30)!

> **4:20** My son, be attentive to my words;
>> incline your ear to my sayings.
> **21** Let them not escape from your sight;
>> keep them within your heart.
> **22** For they are life to those who find them,
>> and healing to all their flesh.
> **23** Keep your heart with all vigilance,
>> for from it flow the springs of life.
> **24** Put away from you crooked speech,
>> and put devious talk far from you.
> **25** Let your eyes look directly forward,
>> and your gaze be straight before you.
> **26** Ponder the path of your feet;
>> then all your ways will be sure.
> **27** Do not swerve to the right or to the left;
>> turn your foot away from evil.

> **10:24** What the wicked dreads will come upon him,
>> but the desire of the righteous will be granted.

> **12:20** Deceit is in the heart of those who devise evil,
>> but those who plan peace have joy.

---

3   Large Catechism I 310.

14:14 The backslider in heart will be filled with the fruit of his ways,

and a good man will be filled with the fruit of his ways.

20:9 Who can say, "I have made my heart pure;

I am clean from my sin"?

22:5 Thorns and snares are in the way of the crooked;

whoever guards his soul will keep far from them.

28:25 A greedy man stirs up strife,

but the one who trusts in the LORD will be enriched.

Mark and Remark

Mark your favorite proverb above and remark why you chose it.

Personalize and Memorize

"Help and be of service to him in keeping it." With the Holy Spirit's help (John 14:26; Romans 8:11), keeping the Ninth Commandment means guarding our hearts, moving from coveting to counting to our blessings. When we're content with what God has given us, then we can help our neighbors keep what God has given them. Analyze all the Ninth Commandment proverbs you previously marked and choose your favorite. Which proverb will help you keep the Ninth Commandment with fear, love, and trust because you are baptized—because you are created in Christ—because God the Father forgives, loves, and treasures you in His Son first? Memorize it. Imagine a moment this week when you'll utilize your proverb. It will be pleasant if you keep it within you, if it is always ready on your lips (Proverbs 22:18).

Heavenly Father, You open Your hand and satisfy the desires of every living creature. Cause us to fear and love You above all things, that our hearts would not covet that which You have given to our neighbors. Rather, lead us to trust in Your provision of daily bread, be content with what You provide, and reject every evil scheme or enticement that would secure for ourselves that which You have given to others. Enable us to serve our neighbors by helping them keep and guard all that You have given to them; through Jesus Christ, our Lord. Amen.[4]

---

4   *Luther's Small Catechism with Explanation,* Ninth and Tenth Commandments, prayer.

CHAPTER 10

THE TENTH COMMANDMENT

You shall not covet your neighbor's wife, or his manservant or maidservant, his ox or donkey, or anything that belongs to your neighbor. *What does this mean?* We should fear and love God so that we do not entice or force away our neighbor's wife, workers, or animals, or turn them against him, but urge them to stay and do their duty.

Deep Memory

Dig deep and ink your First through Ninth Commandment proverbs.

You Shall Not Covet Your Neighbor's Wife

If keeping the Ninth Commandment means respecting the *things* God has given you and your neighbor, keeping the Tenth Commandment means respecting the *relationships* God has given you and your neighbor, especially your neighbor's spouse.

Actions Speak Louder Than Words

Pair and Share

1. What do most men want in a wife? Name the top three qualities.

Pair and Share

2. What do most women want in a husband? Name the top three qualities.

Proverbs 31:10–31 is an acrostic poem. Each new line begins with the next letter of the Hebrew alphabet. But this artistry gets lost in translation. There are two ways to read Proverbs 31 in English. One way is for women to aspire to be the Proverbs 31 woman and for men to aspire to marry the Proverbs 31 woman. Society wants women to have beauty on the surface, but a Proverbs 31 woman is a woman of action: trustworthy, hardworking, strong, wise, kind, generous, dignified, confident; she fears, loves, and trusts in God above all things.

Another way to read Proverbs 31 is to recognize that these qualities of an excellent wife are also the qualities an excellent man should pursue. It feels a little funny for men, but the Bible tells both men and women that they are the *Bride* of Christ (Ephesians 5:25–27). As much as you love your husband or wife, Jesus says your marriage won't last forever (Mark 12:25). Instead, your teeny-tiny marriage paints a picture of the super-duper marriage between Christ and His Church that *will* last forever (Revelation 19:9). Christ gave Himself up for both men and women to present them as His Bride, holy and without blemish (Ephesians 5:27). Since men are members of the Bride of Christ, Proverbs 31 can also portray the excellent man that Christian men, with the Holy Spirit's help (John 14:26), should also aspire to be.

31:10 An excellent wife who can find?
>   She is far more precious than jewels.
11 The heart of her husband trusts in her,
>   and he will have no lack of gain.
12 She does him good, and not harm,
>   all the days of her life.
13 She seeks wool and flax,
>   and works with willing hands.
14 She is like the ships of the merchant;

she brings her food from afar.

¹⁵ She rises while it is yet night

and provides food for her household

and portions for her maidens.

¹⁶ She considers a field and buys it;

with the fruit of her hands she plants a vineyard.

¹⁷ She dresses herself with strength

and makes her arms strong.

¹⁸ She perceives that her merchandise is profitable.

Her lamp does not go out at night.

¹⁹ She puts her hands to the distaff,

and her hands hold the spindle.

²⁰ She opens her hand to the poor

and reaches out her hands to the needy.

²¹ She is not afraid of snow for her household,

for all her household are clothed in scarlet.

²² She makes bed coverings for herself;

her clothing is fine linen and purple.

²³ Her husband is known in the gates

when he sits among the elders of the land.

²⁴ She makes linen garments and sells them;

she delivers sashes to the merchant.

²⁵ Strength and dignity are her clothing,

and she laughs at the time to come.

²⁶ She opens her mouth with wisdom,

and the teaching of kindness is on her tongue.

²⁷ She looks well to the ways of her household

and does not eat the bread of idleness.

²⁸ Her children rise up and call her blessed;

her husband also, and he praises her:

²⁹ "Many women have done excellently,

but you surpass them all."

³⁰ Charm is deceitful, and beauty is vain,

but a woman who fears the LORD is to be praised.

³¹ Give her of the fruit of her hands,

and let her works praise her in the gates.

Personalize and Memorize

"Urge them to stay and do their duty." With the Holy Spirit's help (John 14:26; Romans 8:11), keeping the Tenth Commandment means respecting the relationships God has given you and your neighbor, especially your neighbor's spouse. Rather than coveting our neighbor's spouse, we should seek to become an excellent woman or man who fears the Lord. If we're content with who we are as the forgiven, loved, and cherished Bride of Christ, then we're less likely to entice or force away our neighbor's spouse. Analyze Proverbs 31:10–31 and choose your favorite proverb. Which proverb will help you keep the Tenth Commandment with fear, love, and trust because you are baptized—because you are created in Christ—because God the Father forgives, loves, and treasures you in His Son first? Memorize it. Imagine a moment this week when you'll utilize your proverb. It will be pleasant if you keep it within you, if it is always ready on your lips (Proverbs 22:18).

Holy and merciful God, You have taught us what You would have us do and not do. Pour out Your Holy Spirit on us so that He may bear fruit in our lives and that, remembering Your mercies and Your laws, we may grow in obedience to Your will and in love for You and our neighbor. Help us to follow the example of Your dear Son, Jesus Christ, our Lord, in whose name we pray. Amen.[1]

---

1   *Luther's Small Catechism with Explanation*, The Close of the Commandments, prayer.

ANSWER GUIDE

Preface

1. Answers will vary from "Absence makes the heart grow fonder" to "Home is where the heart is" to "The way to a man's heart is through his stomach."

2. A proverb is a fun, memorable, short, pithy sentence that either states a general truth, gives good advice, or both.

3. If you're in a group, no one needs to air their dirty laundry in public if they don't want to.

4. My mom saying, "There's more than one way to skin a cat," and my dad saying, "A cat in gloves catches no mice," are examples.

5. First Commandment: You shall have no other gods.
   Second Commandment: You shall not misuse the name of the LORD your God.
   Third Commandment: Remember the Sabbath day by keeping it holy.
   Fourth Commandment: Honor your father and your mother.
   Fifth Commandment: You shall not murder.
   Sixth Commandment: You shall not commit adultery.
   Seventh Commandment: You shall not steal.
   Eighth Commandment: You shall not give false testimony against your neighbor.
   Ninth Commandment: You shall not covet your neighbor's house.
   Tenth Commandment: You shall not covet your neighbor's wife, or his manservant or maidservant, his ox or donkey, or anything that belongs to your neighbor.

6. Again, no one needs to air their dirty laundry in public if they don't want to.

7. No one needs to share their answer, but here are two more examples. If Tommy fears, loves, and trusts in money first, more than God, then he will break the Seventh Commandment second, mismanaging money. If Timmy fears, loves, and trusts in sexual pleasure first, more than God, then he will break the Sixth Commandment second, committing adultery.

8. In my vocation, all employees of Concordia University, Nebraska, are expected to respect the official doctrines of the LCMS and to pursue lifestyles that are in moral harmony with its teachings.

9. One man, Adam, messed everything up; one man, Jesus, placed everything in its place (Romans 5:18–19).

10. My students need to study for tests all the time. Pressured by the first use of the Law, they'll study because if they don't, then they'll make a bad grade. Convicted by the second use of the Law, they'll study to make up for a previous bad grade. Guided by the third use of the Law, they will study because they are forgiven, loved, and treasured children of God. Good grades are not the goal of studying. The goal of studying is to master the material so that students can give God's grace to their neighbor in their future vocations.

11. My students study for tests all the time. While they wish their only motive was the Gospel (to be forgiven, loved, and treasured children of God and to give God's grace to others), most of them are also motivated by the first use of the Law (if they don't study, they'd get a bad grade). Since Christians are simultaneously saint and sinner, Christians are often a mixed bag of motives.

12. Sometimes, when we think of Baptism, we think of babies or a longer church service or, worse, that Baptism is "just a symbol."

13. Romans 6 reminds us that Baptism binds us to the crucifixion and resurrection of Jesus. Because Baptism binds us to Christ Jesus, you may consider yourself dead to sin and alive to God in Christ Jesus.

14. Answers will vary, but here are my top three: Each and every action I should do and every single sin I shouldn't do keeps or breaks one of the Ten Commandments. If the First Commandment is kept first, then all the other Commandments shall be kept. A Christian fears, loves, and trusts in God above all things second because God forgives, loves, and treasures him or her first (1 John 4:19).

The First Commandment

1. A (false) god is anything we fear, love, and trust in more than God.

2. A person might be a spouse, boyfriend or girlfriend, or child. A place might be a vacation destination, a man cave, or anywhere people go to get away from it all. A thing might be a smartphone, Netflix, or Cheetos. An idea might be Relativism (man is the measure of all things), Epicureanism (pleasure is the measure of all things), or Materialism (matter is the only thing that matters).

3. A popular proverb says, "Spare the rod, spoil the child." A biblical proverb says the same: "My son, do not despise the LORD's discipline or be weary of His reproof, for the LORD reproves him whom He loves, as a father the son in whom he delights" (Proverbs 3:11–12).

4. God was glad. "The fear of the LORD is the beginning of wisdom" (Proverbs 9:10).

5. No one needs to air their dirty laundry, but here are some more examples. When Tommy skips the Divine Service on Sunday, he has penultimately broken the Third Commandment, but he has ultimately broken the First Commandment, fearing, loving, and trusting in rest and relaxation more than God. When Timmy refuses to call or visit his widowed mother, he has penultimately broken the Fourth Commandment, but he has ultimately broken the First Commandment, fearing, loving, and trusting in his own self-sufficiency more than God.

The Second Commandment

1. For example, my name is David, which means "beloved." Baptized into Christ, I am a beloved child of God (Mark 1:11).

2. Used more than 6,820 times in the Old Testament, YHWH is God's personal name, and it means "I am who I am." There never was a time when YHWH was not, and there never will be a time when YHWH won't be. Jesus means "YHWH saves." Jesus' name matches His messianic work. "He will save His people from their sins" (Matthew 1:21).

The Third Commandment

1. Hiking in the mountains, walking on the beach, long trip, staycation, and so on.

2. Here's a biblical example: Peter did not practice what he preached when he denied Jesus (Matthew 26:33, 74). Peter practiced what he preached in Acts 5 (see especially v. 29).

3. Some healthy habits could include eight hours of sleep each night, daily devotions, exercise, and a healthy breakfast.

The Fourth Commandment

1. James 1:27 says, "Religion that is pure and undefiled before God the Father is this: to visit orphans and widows in their affliction, and to keep oneself unstained from the world."

2. Though many would have thought they were crazy, my parents still paid for my college education, even though I was a philosophy major.

3. Make hay while the sun shines.

4. This controversial topic may open Pandora's box. Different strokes for different folks. Simply accept how different parents choose to discipline their children.

5. Spare the rod, spoil the child. Choose the rod, cherish the child.

6. Some examples are a hair club for men and wrinkle cream for women.

7. My students evaluate me at the midterm and at the end of every semester. Some of the constructive things they say do pinch. A proverb reminds me, "If I can't stand the heat, get out of the kitchen."

8. God instituted the government authorities. They are God's servants for approving the good and avenging the bad.

The Fifth Commandment

1. A table is a piece of furniture with a flat top and legs, providing a level surface on which objects may be placed, that can be used for such purposes as eating, writing, working, or playing games.

2. Whenever I help my neighbor fulfill his functions of fearing, loving, and trusting in God above all things and honoring, loving, and cherishing his neighbor as himself, then I am helping and supporting my neighbor.

3. Anger breaks the Fifth Commandment in thought. Insults break it in word.

4. Since it is hard to hurt those who are helping you, heaping hot coals means to pinch their conscience and push them toward repentance.

The Sixth Commandment

1. Some examples of the "perfect" man from pop culture are Richie Rich, Steady Freddy, and Captain von Trapp. Some for the "perfect" woman might be Wonder Woman, Stable Mable, and Maria von Trapp.

2. They have put the cart before the horse. Without leaving and cleaving first, their hearts are not healthy enough for sex.

3. God created a time and a place for sexual passion in marriage.

The Seventh Commandment

1. Many of us think of bell bottoms, long hair, tie dye, and the like.

2. "Fool! This night your soul is required of you, and the things you have prepared, whose will they be?" (Luke 12:20). "Do not boast about tomorrow, for you do not know what a day may bring" (Proverbs 27:1).

3. "The point is this: whoever sows sparingly will also reap sparingly, and whoever sows bountifully will also reap bountifully. Each one must give as he has decided in his heart, not reluctantly or under compulsion, for God loves a cheerful giver. And God is able to make all grace abound to you, so that having all sufficiency in all things at all times, you may abound in every good work" (2 Corinthians 9:6–8).

4. All people great and small, the Lord God made them all.

5. As you make your bed, so you must lie in it.

The Eighth Commandment

1. A scoffer is someone who expresses scorn, derision, and contempt.

2. "'Scoffer' is the name of the arrogant, haughty man who acts with arrogant pride" (Proverbs 21:24).

3. A biblical example is when the devil victimized Eve with the very first lie: "You will not surely die" (Genesis 3:4).

4. If someone's intent is to hurt or harm, honesty is not always the best policy.

5. We put the cart before the horse. We jump out of the frying pan into the fire.

6. No one needs to air their dirty laundry in public if they don't want to.

The Ninth Commandment

1. No one needs to air their dirty laundry in public if they don't want to.

2. Some things I'm thankful for are coffee, caffeine, cappuccino, coffee shops, and cups of coffee.

3. Many notice that they are thankful for a lot of First Article gifts and that we especially forget about God's Third Article gifts.

4. The Holy Spirit would help our hearts be a little less holey, grateful for all the ways God is gracious to us.

5. Some important decisions include whom to marry, what work to pursue, and where to live.

6. If grumpy neighbors will give gifts to their impudent neighbors and evil fathers will give gifts to their importunate children, "how much more will the heavenly Father give the Holy Spirit to those who ask Him" (Luke 11:13).

The Tenth Commandment

1. At worst, men might look for beauty, charm, and more beauty.

2. At worst, women might look for brawn, brains, and more brawn.

SUMMARY SHEET

The First Commandment: You shall have no other gods.

We should fear, love, and trust in God above all things.

The Second Commandment: You shall not misuse the name of the LORD your God.

We should fear and love God so that we do not curse, swear, use satanic arts, lie, or deceive by His name, but call upon it in every trouble, pray, praise, and give thanks.

The Third Commandment: Remember the Sabbath day by keeping it holy.

We should fear and love God so that we do not despise preaching and His Word, but hold it sacred and gladly hear and learn it.

The Fourth Commandment: Honor your father and your mother.

We should fear and love God so that we do not despise or anger our parents and other authorities, but honor them, serve and obey them, love and cherish them.

The Fifth Commandment: You shall not murder.

We should fear and love God so that we do not hurt or harm our neighbor in his body, but help and support him in every physical need.

The Sixth Commandment: You shall not commit adultery.

We should fear and love God so that we lead a sexually pure and decent life in what we say and do, and husband and wife love and honor each other.

The Seventh Commandment: You shall not steal.

We should fear and love God so that we do not take our neighbor's money or possessions, or get them in any dishonest way, but help him to improve and protect his possessions and income.

The Eighth Commandment: You shall not give false testimony against your neighbor.

We should fear and love God so that we do not tell lies about our neighbor, betray him, slander him, or hurt his reputation, but defend him, speak well of him, and explain everything in the kindest way.

The Ninth Commandment: You shall not covet your neighbor's house.

We should fear and love God so that we do not scheme to get our neighbor's inheritance or house, or get it in a way which only appears right, but help and be of service to him in keeping it.

The Tenth Commandment: You shall not covet your neighbor's wife, or his manservant or maidservant, his ox or donkey, or anything that belongs to your neighbor.

We should fear and love God so that we do not entice or force away our neighbor's wife, workers, or animals, or turn them against him, but urge them to stay and do their duty.